Fathering Through Divorce

A Handbook for Men Dealing with Divorce and its Impact on Parenting

Produced by Men Mentoring Men
Written by Carol Patton

(menmentoringmen.org)

Note for Librarians: A cataloguing record for this book is available from Library
and Archives Canada at www.collectionscanada.ca/amicus/index-e.html

Printed in Victoria, BC, Canada.

ISBN: 978-1-4269-1708-0 (sc)

*Our mission is to efficiently provide the world's finest, most comprehensive book publishing
service, enabling every author to experience success. To find out how to publish your book, your
way, and have it available worldwide, visit us online at www.trafford.com*

Trafford rev. 10/02/2009

 www.trafford.com

North America & international
toll-free: 1 888 232 4444 (USA & Canada)
phone: 250 383 6864 ♦ fax: 812 355 4082

DEDICATION

MY FATHER, IRV Greenberg (1916-2008) lived a long healthy life surrounded by good friends, loving family, a wonderful sense of humor; who aged gracefully accepting his frailties, and exited this earthly world with dignity. I cannot think of a more fitting and rewarding life. Despite his usual wry comment of "only the good go young", he was a good guy and lived a long enriching life.

His life wasn't always so easy and wonderful. Irv was born and grew up near Harlem, then the south Bronx. He went to NYC public schools and graduated from CCNY. He was in the Coast Guard during WW II serving as a meteorologist sending up weather balloons over the North Atlantic to prepare for the Normandy invasion. General Eisenhower counted on Irv's advice, as did many others and I years later. After the war, he joined the National Weather Bureau and traveled around the Northeast doing weather forecasting before there were computer models. He later transferred to the FDA. He married my Mother in 1949, had 2 children, in 1950 and 1955; and then joined the pharmaceutical industry as a 'detail man', who called on doctors to describe their new medicines. Some would consider this a sales job, but Irv saw it more as 'education' or a teaching position. My parents divorced in 1961, though Irv re-married in 1963 and settled in Queens, where he resided until his death. He spent most of his career working for AH Robins/Wyeth, and worked part-time well into his 70s, while he attended college classes well into his 80s.

At 46 years old, Irv found himself divorced with a bitter ex-wife, and 2 small children ages 11 and 6, living with his recently widowed Mother in order to meet his child support and alimony obligations. I don't ever recall him complaining or doubting his priorities. In recent years, seeing my friends go through divorce and especially being part of Men Mentoring Men and hearing the details of what single dads go through do I realize what his life in those harried years must have been like. It was with those realizations that the thought of producing this handbook as a contribution to men, and a memorial tribute to Irv's life became a reality. I think Irv would love the thought of assisting his fellow man while providing some guidance and nurturing. He would approve of showing men that you can emerge from the other side of a divorce rebuilt and happy.

Irv loved people and kibitzing. He enjoyed his kids and especially his grandkids, though he enjoyed a conversation with almost anyone about almost anything. He had an easy, calm demeanor and smile. All I know who met him enjoyed his company.

When he was in his final days, he thanked me for all I had done and was doing for him. Upon reflection, I was dumbfounded to think of all he sacrificed of his life, all he provided to me to always feel safe, secure, accepted and loved, with comfort, support, guidance, and abundant education; and here he was thanking me! I still struggle with understanding and accepting this comment. Therefore, I dedicate this book to Irv Greenberg as a memorial to his life and one way of me saying, "Thank You, Pops!"

Dr. Howard Greenberg – Men Mentoring Men Trustee

ACKNOWLEDGEMENTS

W E WOULD LIKE to thank our writer, Carol Patton, for her extraordinary effort in researching, interviewing and writing of the handbook. Her sensitivity and intelligence are reflected in all aspects of the project.

We would also like to thank all of the people and organizations that donated their time, expertise and wisdom to this handbook. Likewise, a special thank you to the men who shared their amazing stories that were filled with courage, insight and emotion and to the committee, which championed the project. Your collected efforts have helped us produce a powerful resource for men all around this country who are going through the painful process of divorce and parenting after divorce.

To the men reading this guidebook: It is our hope that your life will soon be filled with love and happiness. You will survive. You will have an opportunity to learn, an opportunity to grow. In the end, you may be a better person for demonstrating your strength, integrity and compassion while traveling down this difficult road.

The men of Men Mentoring Men

Contents

INTRODUCTION

YOU NEVER THOUGHT this day would come, that your marriage would fall apart. You were so happy, so much in love with each other. What happened? How did you end up this way? What went so wrong?

Any way you look at it, divorces are never easy. Yet, despite everything you're feeling and experiencing, you can't afford to stay stuck in neutral. Now is the time to move, to take action, to be intelligent, compassionate and prepared. This isn't only for your benefit but to perhaps ensure a stable and happy future for your children.

So what should you do? Whom should you call? What's your first step?

Men Mentoring Men (M3) offers this guidebook as a way to help you navigate through the emotional and sometimes complicated process of divorce. Our New Jersey-based nonprofit organization is dedicated to helping men of all ages, backgrounds and cultures, survive personal traumas as well as celebrate their accomplishments, no matter how big or small.

Each chapter in this handbook offers resources and tips from experts around the country as well as real stories and insights from men who have gone through this painful experience.

It is our goal to make you whole again, to help you move forward with your life, smiling, laughing, and enjoying whatever may come your way. Divorce is not the end but simply a marker of a major change in your life. Ultimately, it's your choice which direction you take. We encourage you to use this guidebook to help plot a personal course that leads you toward a happy and fulfilling future.

CHAPTER 1:

Accepting the Reality of Divorce

MUCH HAS BEEN written and said about divorce. You can hardly watch TV or read a newspaper without learning about someone's steamy affair, huge alimony settlement or grueling custody case. These days, divorce has become synonymous with the word marriage and almost as ubiquitous as drinking an ice-cold beer on a hot summer day.

The only thing that divorces have in common is that they are a painful process - mentally, emotionally and financially. A husband finds out his wife cheated on him, no longer loves him or simply wants to regain her single status. Or perhaps he finds his life lacking and simply wants to move on. Any way you look at it, it hurts, badly.

Men sometimes express their feelings about divorce to close family members or friends. Others announce them to the world. Consider these emotions posted by men on a divorce blog:

- I feel like a failure because I couldn't make it work.
- I feel guilty - I must have done something wrong to cause our divorce.
- My heart aches.
- I'm bitter and angry because of what I had to go through.
- I'm insecure about my future.
- I was badly burned.
- I'm lost and don't know what to do next.
- I feel like I've been skinned alive.
- I'm terrified about what's going to happen to me.
- My emotions are raw.
- I feel like a huge knot being pulled through a tiny hole.

These are all legitimate feelings. Have you come to terms with your own? You may feel angry, resentful or possibly embarrassed. Or maybe you're still numb. Either way, you must recognize and effectively deal with your emotions before you can accept your divorce.

Forget the promises once made or the trust once assumed. Love and relationships are fluid, rarely staying the same from moment to moment. Denial will only delay your ability to get past this difficult stage in your life. You need to move on. You deserve to be happy. Now is the time – not tomorrow - to start feeling good about yourself again.

So say the words that you never thought you would have to utter:

"I am getting a divorce."

Shout them, maybe more than once. It may offer you a sense of relief and peace. It's an easy way to release very strong emotions that you're carrying around inside of you every minute of every day. They are excess baggage that can only make your days more difficult and harder for you to develop future, healthy relationships.

Then cut yourself some slack. Give yourself permission to feel good. It's OK. Really. Do something that makes you feel good. Do things that you avoided while you were married because your wife disapproved of them. Maybe play golf on Saturday and Sunday. Do something adventurous. Take a class on whatever interests you. It really doesn't matter what you do as long as you do something. That's when you can begin to climb out of this seemingly deep, dark, endless hole called divorce.

Reaching Out

Oftentimes, men accept personal responsibility for their divorce. Some feel guilty or ashamed, blaming themselves for not being able to maintain a happy and healthy relationship. No matter what the underlying causes were – even if the divorce is mutual – they believe their divorce is a reflection of their inability to manage or control their life and develop self-esteem issues.

Some men are so ashamed that they place a shield around themselves, not allowing anyone to get close enough to talk to about their feelings or situation, says Marion Solomon, a licensed social worker and marriage and family therapist in Los Angeles who has counseled men going through divorce. In their mind, what are they going to say? My wife found me inadequate? My wife found someone she loved more? They internalize their feelings, believing something is wrong with them.

She tells the story of one of her patients, a successful businessman, who lived in a hotel for a short period of time following his divorce. He never told anyone at work about his divorce or feelings of loss and despair. He would go to his office every day, return to his hotel room at night, feeling so alone and vulnerable, and cry. Then in the morning, he would pull himself together and start the same routine all over again.

Even men who leave their wife for another woman may still feel terrible about their divorce. Solomon says they often justify it by saying they would have left anyway, that the woman waiting in the wings had nothing to do with their decision to leave. Still, they were the ones to quit. They couldn't find a way to make their marriage work.

Regardless of your feelings, Solomon says among the worst things you can do is to isolate yourself. Don't cut off friends or family members who care about you. Invite them into your world no matter how much pain or misery exists. Or make new friends who can support you through this difficult time.

Back in 2000, a study published in the Journal of Epidemiology and Community Health discovered that divorced and separated men were two and a half times more likely to end their life by suicide than married men. The researcher theorized that unlike men, women form deep personal friendships or social support networks that help them get through tough times like divorce.

So take the first step. Surround yourself with people who care. Volunteer for a worthy cause. Join a gym or professional association. Seek counseling from a therapist, social worker, psychologist or psychiatrist. Find a support group. You'll discover that you're not alone. Many other men are feeling the same kinds of emotions and perhaps are struggling just as hard as you are to move forward. Sharing your feelings and concerns with men who are experiencing the same kind of emotional challenges can be very cathartic and often liberating.

The key is not to make your divorce a stopping point in your life, says Solomon. Life never stands still so why should you? She says some men just go through the motions of living but stop being themselves and doing the things they enjoy. It's like they're punishing themselves for something that may have been beyond their control. They allow the trauma of divorce to take over almost every aspect of their life, preventing themselves from being happy or productive.

While there's no set timetable for healing, don't let your pain drag on and on until you're completely drained, void of any feelings or become ill. Solomon says it can take several months before your anger or fears dissipate, which is all a normal part of the healing process. But don't stay stuck in neutral or worse, go in reverse. If you haven't made any progress within a reasonable amount of time for your situation, become more angry or depressed as time goes on, or haven't found any relief from your pain, then you may have unresolved issues or unfinished business that you should address with a professional therapist.

There are many different avenues or resources for help. Many divorced men get involved in support groups, which can be extremely valuable. However, be careful of those whose members are more interested in repeatedly playing the role of victim, trashing their ex-wives or sharing horror stories than in moving forward. Although it may feel good to vent by saying bad things about your ex-wife, how horrible she treated you or the lousy things she did to you, there comes a time when you must stop and shift gears. Otherwise, you end up spinning your wheels in the mud. Nothing gets resolved. Nothing gets accomplished. Your anger just perpetuates itself with no end in sight.

Just as important, pay attention to things that may trigger your anger, depression or other negative emotions and cause you to over-react, even explode, over minor situations at work or home, adds Halcy Bohen, a licensed psychologist in Washington, DC.

Contact with your ex-wife or soon-to-be ex can be huge triggers. If she says something infuriating to you over the phone, tell her you need to call back in 20 minutes, explains Bohen. Make up a reason like someone's knocking at your front door. Get off the phone as quickly as possible before you lose your temper or say something you'll regret. Likewise, don't fire off responses to her emails right away.

"You can spew all you want, just don't hit send," says Bohen. While in a fit of anger, you may write something that you'll regret or could possibly be used against you down the road. So store the email in a safe place, then look at it after you've calmed down. But if you're bursting with anger, ask someone you trust, like a friend or colleague, to review it with you, then decide whether or not to send it, edit it or toss it.

Other common triggers can be those that remind you of good or bad times with your ex-wife. A scene in a movie, a restaurant or song can bring back loving or painful memories. So can your children who share stories with you about how much fun they have with their mother. Maybe she took them shopping, to the zoo or movies, or buys them nice gifts.

Bohen says hearing anything pleasant about your ex-wife can trigger hurt feelings, rage or other strong emotions. If she was the one to hurt you, you don't want to hear that she's happy or successful at anything right now—even if it involves your children. Recognize this before you talk with her. Or, when talking with your children, shift the focus from how much fun they had with your ex-wife at the zoo to visiting the zoo with them through their eyes - what animals did they see, did the lions scare them or what did they learn about monkeys. By being prepared or expecting strong emotions to surface, you can better cope with whatever comes along.

However, if you're the one who asked for the divorce, expect your ex-wife to have similar feelings toward you. Don't be surprised if she becomes angry and you can't figure out what you said or did to cause the outburst. Be supportive but reasonable. Help her in any way you can but don't enable her to have false hopes. If every time something breaks in the house that you once both shared, and you drop everything to run over and fix it, realize that she may be trying to lure you back into a potentially dead-end relationship.

If you periodically receive angry or confusing emails from her, recognize that she is going through a difficult situation and that the messages may have been written during a moment when she just needed to vent her anger, fear or frustrations about the divorce. Don't let them stir up your emotions or provoke your anger.

While every couple is different, every divorce is different, but there is one rule that can never, ever be broken. Don't speak negatively about your ex-wife to your children or be angry with them because they have a good relationship with her. Verbal attacks or trash talk make it miserable for everyone, especially your children, and can cause them emotional harm in the long run.

Bohen says anger almost always covers more vulnerable emotions like fear or a sense of abandonment.

"Those more vulnerable emotions for all of us, usually connect back to vulnerable feelings when we were younger," she says. "If you can figure out those connections, it can help you a lot in going forward. But just to storm around with the anger and leave it at that [or worse], act it out with the ex, is a recipe that is no good for anybody."

So be aware of the circumstances right before your blood begins to boil or feelings of sorrow or loss spill over into other portions of your life. Write them down, then look at them later to figure out why your reaction was so strong. Why did it affect you so hard? Why did it make you so upset or depressed? Once you understand why these events set off such strong emotions, you can be better equipped to deal with them next time around and learn how to control your behavior.

Consider using a professional therapist when you can no longer control your emotions or feel as if you'll never regain control of them. Likewise, therapy can help if your negative feelings seem to go on and on and you lack the psychological tools to move ahead. There are many categories of therapists to choose from. Work with them to help you move beyond your anger and control other negative emotions. If you feel hurt or that you've been wronged in any way, they can help you identify what role you played in the whole process leading up to and through your divorce.

Bohen says there are everyday things you may have done like not listening to what your ex-wife wanted to talk about or not sharing the responsibilities, everything from raising your children to taking out the garbage. But if the roles were reversed where you were the real sweetheart and she was the abuser or neglecter, it's still important to ask yourself why you tolerated the relationship for as long as you did.

"Without that self-examination of what didn't go right, you're bound to repeat it," she says. "Even if you think the next person you find is totally different from your first wife, chances are you'll make those mistakes again unless you've done a really careful examination of your own part, your own early issues that may have played out in the relationship."

Avoiding the Danger Zone

Every person handles the side effects of divorce differently. It depends upon his circumstance. You may know someone who is simply devastated, still deeply in love with his wife, and is even having trouble performing daily tasks. He is obsessed with his loss and almost feels like he is mourning the death of a loved one. And in reality, he is mourning, not an individual, but the death of his marriage and a way of life that he once treasured.

Yet, another person may actually be relieved, feeling liberated because he got out of what he considered to be a bad situation. Maybe he was stuck in a loveless marriage, feeling that the marriage did not add to the quality of his life and probably held him back in some ways. Or he just grew tired of constantly bickering with his wife over trivial things. Love and support may have been replaced with confrontation and roadblocks to moving forward.

While every individual is entitled to his own feelings, they may differ from yours. Don't use their feelings as a measuring stick for your own emotions or a guideline for coping with your unique situation. Pay special attention to what you're feeling. Even the smoothest of divorces have rocky moments that can trigger a landslide of negative emotions like anger, frustration, hopelessness, or sorrow and despair.

This is why during divorce proceedings, some couples can easily divide up all their earthly possessions in less than an hour. Yet, they can be involved in several months of harsh bickering and negotiation to decide who gets custody of their Rolling Stones Greatest Hits CD. It's not that the item is valuable to either of them. It's just being used as a vehicle to express and release all of their pent up emotions.

Despite what your ex-wife or her mother or friends might say, you're not a robot. You're just as vulnerable and just as likely as anyone else to react to a wide variety of emotions following a divorce, ranging from fear to freedom.

The problem starts when an individual loses control. He no longer has the ability to manage his feelings, which leads to a series of negative thoughts that never seem to end. No matter what he does to get rid of them, they haunt him.

His inability to get rid of these negative thoughts can result in some pretty radical behavioral changes, which are attempts to get rid of his negative thoughts. Like a dog chasing its tail, it just goes round and round. His world spirals out of control and he doesn't know how to stop it.

Try hard not to fall into this trap. There will be many days where you may feel angry, irritable or depressed. Expect it. It's actually quite normal. In fact, embrace those negative emotions. Know that they're a normal part of the healing process. Only then will you be able to let go of them and move on. It's just like building a new house after the walls of your old house have fallen down around you. You can't build new walls until you've built a strong foundation.

The warning signs are everywhere. Some are very obvious while others are almost invisible. Have you stopped caring about your appearance? Is your house or apartment a total mess? Have you washed your car in the last three months? Have you lost interest in activities you used to enjoy? Do you have problems sleeping or concentrating on routine tasks at work or home? Did you eat dinner today? How about yesterday? Are you avoiding your friends? Most importantly, are you even aware if these things are happening in your life? These invisible demons can cause just as much pain as the ones that walk through your front door.

Everybody copes in different ways. The magic is in knowing your situation, recognizing your denial and defining the work you need to do to move on to a more positive place in your life.

Richard

After 26 years of marriage, Richard's wife asked him for a divorce. At the time, Richard was also suing his employer for wrongful dismissal. Approximately 15 months into his rocky, 18-month, public lawsuit, she could no longer tolerate its ups and downs or their marriage. His life at work and home had fallen apart.

Looking back, Richard felt betrayed. While his relationship wasn't ideal or even a great marriage, he says it was nonetheless a stable marriage.

"I can accept the fact that in a marriage love dissipates but here was someone I considered to be my best friend," he says. "I've been there for her, brought three children with her into the world, raised them and shared other things in life. And now when I was finally at the bottom and needed all the help I could get, my best friend and partner wasn't there to support me. It was devastating."

Richard's anger over her decision to end their marriage also grew over time. But he was even madder at her attempt to kick him out of his own home where his three children lived. He knew he would survive the divorce, however, the thought of not living with his children was brutal. At the time, two of his children were in high school while the third was in middle school. He was an involved dad and enjoyed playing an active role in their lives.

But due to his job loss and mounting legal expenses – he lost the lawsuit - moving wasn't even an option. At least, not now, which is what he told his wife. He couldn't afford to move. Plain and simple.

So for the next eight months, he and his wife shared the same house with their children. Richard slept in the upstairs master bedroom while his wife chose to sleep on the couch in the downstairs family room. His paternal instincts to help raise his children and protect them were what kept him sane. He says they were his primary, guiding light through this entire process.

Despite his anger or hostility toward his wife, he kept his emotions at bay, never allowing his children to witness his anger. He and his wife basically performed the same daily routine as in the past – everything from eating meals together to driving their children to and from school and sports-related activities. But over time, they became complete strangers. There was no more physical or emotional intimacy. No more hope of reconciliation. No more relationship. They both knew divorce was inevitable, he says.

"In my mind, I was over it, she was over it and I wasn't going to put emotional energy into dealing with her," he says. "I was in a pretty angry state but deep down, I knew that life wasn't going to come to an end. My thought was once you've hit bottom and survive, you're going to come out if it and nothing else will ever get you."

He says when going through divorce, you must deal with the situation at hand, regardless of what emotions you're feeling or how much pain you're experiencing. Hiding your head in the sand just makes it worse. He says there's no way to avoid the pain associated with a divorce so you might as well move toward it, feel it, work through it and come out on the other side. While no one looks forward to such challenges, he says the longer you put it off or push it aside, the more pain you may feel and the longer it will take you to get back to a place of normalcy and be happy again.

Part of Richard's coping strategies also included dating. It had been more than 20 years since he had been out on a date. Although just the thought of it made him nervous and anxious, he needed to know that he was still capable of forming relationships with other women. So he started dating after several months, but never shared his experiences with his children or discussed it with his wife.

But being human, Richard says his "dark side" did appear on occasion. While living together could have spurred numerous arguments and potentially turn violent, Richard would not allow his anger to take control, destroy him or his family. Instead, he found more subtle ways of expressing his anger.

He still laughs every time he thinks about it. After returning from a date at two o'clock or three o'clock in the morning, he always parked his car in the garage, never in the driveway, and entered his house through the garage, never the front door. The family room where his wife slept was above the garage. So he knew the sound of the garage door opening would wake up her and perhaps leave her wondering where he had been and with whom until the early hours of the morning. The thought always left a smile on his face.

Although seemingly minimal, acts like this are often harmless and a way to relieve tension or anger. Don't be surprised if thoughts like this cross your mind. It's perfectly normal to have these feelings and strike back at the one who hurt you. Just be careful that it doesn't get out hand and create greater problems for you than already exist.

Richard says the loss of power over his life or inability to control it led to fear, then anger. When angry, he said he felt-righteous and powerful. But as time wore on, he realized the destructive nature of anger and searched for others ways to empower himself.

Little by little, as Richard regained control of his life, his fear slowly disappeared. He felt confident that he could handle whatever came his way.

There was no more reason to be that angry and he could move forward without any old, self-imposed restraints.

Seven years after his divorce, Richard remarried. He wrote a book on parenting, started a relationship coaching business with his new wife and also runs a nonprofit agency that deals with children and families who are facing behavioral and mental health challenges.

"Being proactive gave me a sense of control over my life, helped me channel away from anger and restored my sense of personal power," he says, an active member of M3.

Greg

At age 39, Greg found different ways to regain his personal power. After being married for 17 years, participating in marriage, individual and group counseling, and learning that his wife had engaged in an extramarital relationship, he finally filed for divorce.

Unlike Richard's wife, Greg's wife voluntarily moved out of the house, leaving him to predominantly raise their three children who ranged between the ages of nine and 14.

Since his young children required supervision, he stayed home after work and found effective ways to cope with his new situation. After his children went to bed at night, he began journaling his feelings and daily experiences.

"It helped me because it was forcing me to begin my internal journey," says Greg, also a member of M3. "I was analyzing who I was and figuring out what I had to do and how I could do it. I knew how to be a father but didn't know how to be a mother and a father. I was terrified."

But Greg wouldn't allow his fears to paralyze him from moving forward. He read many self-improvement books, which he says helped him better deal with his emotions and experience personal growth, and became entrenched in cultural activities, even taking an art course. He also added exercise to his daily routine, taking long walks, jogging, bike-riding and lifting weights. While all of this helped him through this difficult time, it was his psychologist who gave him the key to his future.

"I turned off the spigot," he says, explaining that his ex-wife still called *him for advice on everything from fixing the faucet to fixing her love life. "I stopped being her resource and confidant, her sounding board. I also did the same thing with her family members. It was a tremendous relief."*

When she called, he simply followed his therapist's advice: he politely listened to her, asked if she was finished talking, then told her he was going to hang up the phone. After six or seven phone calls, she finally got the message, he says, adding that this technique helped diffuse some of his anger.

Greg, now 59 years-old, never remarried. However, he has had several long-term, healthy relationships with women and now lives with a woman he has been involved with for almost four years.

He's since forgiven his wife for her indiscretions. But most importantly, he has forgiven himself for actually filing for divorce, admitting that some part of him still loves his ex-wife.

Looking back, he says it took more than six years before he could close this chapter in his life.

"After gaining a little more perspective as a divorced, single man, I finally realized that the sun still rises, the moon still come ups and the sky is still blue."

What Type of Therapist Is Right For You?

If you're seeking help to put your divorce behind you, there are just as many types of therapists to choose from as there are treatment approaches. Here is a brief listing of clinical professions and approaches that may be useful.

Your first task is to find which level of therapy best meets your needs. Keep in mind that you're not limited to just one type of therapy. Some men find it helpful to participate in individual counseling and group therapy at the same time.

Remember, you're in control of this process and like buying a car, the first salesman you talk to may not be the best one for you. Each therapist and approach has advantages and disadvantages so search until you find the best possible match. Find someone you're comfortable with, who challenges you and makes you think about what's happening in your life without making you defensive. If you meet someone who simply agrees with everything you say, that will not help you move in any direction – good or bad. The purpose of seeing a therapist is to form a trusting relationship where you can comfortably make changes, try new things and feel good about yourself.

Psychiatrists are physicians who are medically trained in psychiatry to diagnose and treat mental disorders. They prescribe drugs, such as anti-depressants, to help you deal with clinical or situational depression, or other mental health disorders. While psychiatrists can help you overcome strong emotions related to your divorce, their primary focus is really to provide drugs that interact with your brain function to alleviate some of your emotional pain. However, they are highly unlikely to spend an hour talking with you to find solutions to your divorce-related problems. That task is left to other disciplines.

Clinical Psychologists study how people think, act and behave. While some focus on research, others deal primarily with patients. Many have a doctoral degree in psychology or related field and are licensed by their state, but they are not physicians. Most can't prescribe drugs or medication. If you turn to a clinical psychologist for help, they'll spend time talking with you to evaluate your situation and your needs. Then they'll identify ways you can change your thoughts or behaviors to get rid of negative emotions like fear over your divorce or anger directed at your ex-wife, so you can move forward with your life and avoid repeating past mistakes in future relationships.

Clinical Social Workers have a college degree in social work. Some also have advanced degrees, either a master's degree or doctorate, and their licensing depends upon their level of education. They assist people by helping them cope with day-to-day issues, deal with their relationships, and solve personal and family problems. They spend a great deal of time talking with you and developing a plan of action to help you deal with your divorce.

Counselors, in some states, do not have to be licensed. Watch out for those who may lack the necessary experience or training. Work with a counselor who is a licensed professional. Their primary focus is to help you understand and address your divorce-related problems. They are very likely to work with you to develop a step-by-step plan that takes you from where you are to where you need or want to be. As you reach your defined goals, they will assist you in developing new goals and new directions to make sure you continue the process of growth.

Support Groups may be led by a trained therapist but some are run by people who are just experiencing the same situation as you are. Each group focuses on a specific life challenge like divorce, death or addiction, and can attract all men, all women or both genders of different ages and backgrounds. If you join a support group just for men, for instance, you can easily bond with other members, form new friendships and share mutual experiences and survival tips that are more appropriate for men. However, by joining a mixed support group, you'll gain the woman's perspective, which may help you better understand your ex-wife's feelings and behaviors.

Now there are many online support groups as well. While it's helpful to vent your feelings, stay away from sites whose members routinely bash women, constantly complain and are more focused on venting their anger than personal growth.

Coaches, who are sometimes referred to as personal or life coaches, don't have to be certified to practice this profession. They can help you manage difficult changes, develop new skills and deal with a wide variety of challenges ranging from coping with stress to achieving balance in your life. Coaches tend to focus less on emotions and more on setting goals and identifying behaviors that help you reach those goals. When working with an effective or experienced coach, you may become more self-aware or develop a better understanding of who you are, where you want to go and how to get there.

Need Help?

Contact any of these support groups or organizations for help or information:

Men Mentoring Men
www.mthree.org/site/

Divorce Care
www.divorcecare.org

Divorce Care for Kids
www.dc4k.org/parentzone

American Coalition for Fathers & Children
www.acfc.org

Listing of support groups by state
divorcehq.com/supportgroups.shtml

Free Divorce Support for Men
www.freedivorcesupportformen.com

National Directory of Psychologists
www.psychologyinfo.com/directory/

National Directory of mental wellness professionals providing eTherapy
and Therapy Chat on the Net
www.etherapyweb.com/state.html

Parents without Partners
www.parentswithoutpartners.org

National Association of Social Workers
www.socialworkers.org

Did you know?

1. Nearly half of all marriages end in divorce.
2. Two-thirds of all divorces are initiated by women.
3. After a divorce, 52 percent of men remarry compared to almost 44 percent of women.
4. The US has the world's highest marriage and divorce rate.
5. On average, first marriages that ended in divorce in 2004 lasted about eight years.
6. In 2004, the median time between divorce and a second marriage was about three and one-half years.
7. In 2004, 12 percent of men and 13 percent of women had married twice, and three percent each had married three or more times.

CHAPTER 2 -

Taking Care of Business

Expect the unexpected.

T HESE THREE LITTLE words should be your mantra as you go
through the process of divorce. When it comes to divorce, the only
thing you can count on is change.

That's why you need to manage whatever is within your control. It will
also help you avoid becoming a victim. Don't wait until your wife drains
your savings account or maxes out your joint credit cards. No matter how
upset you are, how angry or depressed you may be, or how much you
want to move out of the house, put your emotions aside. Now is the time
to take care of business to protect yourself and your children. If you do
things right from the beginning, they'll be less hell to pay in the end.

Before taking any action, find a good, reputable divorce attorney. Ask
your friends or relatives if they know of someone. If that doesn't work,
contact your local BAR association for referrals. Don't choose the first
lawyer you come across. Interview at least two, maybe three. Although it
may cost several hundreds of dollars for each consultation, it's money well
spent. You need an experienced lawyer you can trust, who knows his or
her way around the legal system and has your best interest at heart.

Here are a few questions to ask:

1. What percentage of the law firm is devoted to family law?
    Are the attorneys at the firm jack-of-all-trades and master of none?
    They may not have the experience you need or be distracted by
    other legal issues. More than half of the practice should be devoted
    to family law.

2. How many years of experience does the lawyer have in handling just divorce cases? If you broke your arm, would you see a cardiologist? The same principle applies here. Don't select a criminal attorney or ask your cousin or neighbor who specializes in personal injury to represent you. Hire a lawyer who handles mostly or exclusively divorce cases. This is even more important if your situation is complex like those involving a large estate or perhaps sticky custody/visitation issues. The more years of experience your attorney has working in family law, the better. While it never hurts to shop around, keep in mind that the best referrals often come from other lawyers.

3. How do you get along with the attorney? Your attorney will learn intimate details about you, your ex-wife and your marriage. Developing a good rapport is essential. You must trust your lawyer and have confidence that he or she will produce the best outcome for you. Listen to your gut-instincts.

4. What's the attorney's work style and client philosophy? Do you want to be involved in every aspect of your divorce or in only those things that require your input or feedback? Some attorneys update their clients only when necessary while others educate them along the way, contacting them about all proceedings, discussions and negotiations. Select the attorney that best matches your style or preference. Likewise, clashing personalities is also a sign of trouble. Watch out if the attorney is overly abrasive or aggressive with you, your ex-wife or promotes more problems in your marriage to rack up additional fees. The last thing you need right now is unnecessary stress. So find an attorney you feel comfortable with, someone whose work style, values and ethics are consistent with your own.

5. What are the attorney's fees? Think about each of the attorneys you interviewed. What do you like about them? What do you dislike? Rank them in order of preference. Then consider their fees. Are they reasonable? Can you afford them? The lawyer with the cheapest fees may not be the best way to go. Inexperience often results in costly mistakes that may haunt you for years to come. You could even pay more in the long run than if you hired an experienced attorney. Bottom line: For the most part, better and more experienced lawyers cost more so choose the

most experienced divorce attorney that you can afford who best matches your personality and needs.

Protect Your Assets, Credit Rating and Sanity

Once you've selected your attorney, focus on stabilizing your finances. Some lawyers suggest withdrawing funds from all joint accounts so you can control how the money is spent, ensuring that joint debt like your mortgage, credit cards and utilities are paid off. Other attorneys suggest withdrawing 50 percent of the account's funds since wives are entitled to the other half.

"I always advise my clients to control the accounts," explains Charles "Rusty" Webb, a divorce attorney at The Webb Law Firm in Charleston, W. Va. "To not do that, you're facing the unknown."

Count on your wife's lawyer advising her to do the same. If she's not responsible with money, or is angry and vindictive, he says checks may start bouncing, causing even the best credit scores to plunge in a very short period of time.

It's always better if you temporarily control your joint finances to prevent bad financial decisions from being made. But tell your wife you've drained the accounts. Don't risk her wrath by keeping her in the dark. Let her know you'll be paying all of the bills plus giving her money every week or so for daily needs, such as gas and groceries. Then follow through. No judge wants to hear that your kids didn't have enough to eat because you either seized or squandered your family's savings.

The next task may sound sacrilegious but is necessary in some cases. If possible, cut up the credit cards that you're responsible for or close the accounts, says Webb. Call your credit card companies to explain your situation. Tell them you will not authorize any more purchases. It's a drastic measure but sometimes, well worth it. It's not uncommon for spouses to want to get even by running up the credit card balance, especially if they feel they've been wronged or harmed in some way.

"But any charges run up after separation are the responsibility of the party who ran up the charges," he says. "Usually, courts make those parties responsible if it just looks like they were doing it out of spite."

Even after your divorce, it's still a good idea to be in control of paying any bills or loans that your name appears on, to control credit issues that may arise. Since banks are not always bound by a divorce order, Webb suggests asking the court's permission to pay all bills directly, then deduct that amount from your monthly spousal or child support payment.

As an example, say your ex-wife stays home to raise your children and gets your house in the divorce settlement. Each month, the court has ordered you to give her a support check for $3,000 covering all expenses. Out of that check, she is supposed to pay the mortgage and car payment, totaling $1600. But that may not always happen. If she is irresponsible, her payments may be late or she may use the money for something else. Webb suggests that you pay the $1600 to the creditors and give your ex-wife a check for the remaining $1400 each month. Only pay debt with your name on it. This way, you are still in control of your finances and equally important, your credit.

Ideally, Webb says both husband and wife should refinance, seeking car loans, home mortgages or credit cards in their own name, but that's easier said than done. If your wife doesn't work, she may not be able to secure credit on her own.

Another tip is to claim your children as dependents on your income tax. Federal law says that if you provide 50 percent or more of their support, then you're entitled to the dependency exemption, continues Webb. But state laws, which vary, always trump federal law. In West Virginia, for instance, he says the parent who can claim the tax dependency is the primary residential parent or the parent who is living with the children. However, if the parent is unemployed or a stay-at-home mom, then the husband can use the tax credit.

If pensions are involved, avoid liquidation at all costs because both you and your ex-wife will take huge hits on income tax and penalties. Instead, roll over her share into a qualified retirement plan so there are no tax consequences for either of you. You can also ask your 401(k) plan to cut your ex-wife a check. She'll have a certain number of days to reinvest those funds into a qualified plan, otherwise, she'll have to pay the taxes and penalties on it – not you. Regardless of how bitter your divorce is, Webb says try to avoid paying unnecessary taxes or penalties.

Any good divorce attorney will inform you of your rights and help protect your finances and credit rating. The key is not to fly solo. Get professional legal advice before you take your first step.

Peter

When Peter filed for divorce in 1991, he didn't move fast enough. At the time, his wife of 10 years, who was a homemaker, drained their joint checking account and also secured a line of credit, which was also quickly spent. Then she would do spiteful things. One summer day, she opened all the windows in the house and turned on the air conditioning full blast. Another time, *after Peter discontinued the cable service, she threw away both converter boxes, which cost him $200 each.*

By then, Peter had already moved out of their newly built 2,500 square-foot house but was hardly living in luxury. He rented a room in someone else's apartment so he could live near his children, then attempted reconciliation with his wife, which failed. He moved several more times over the next five or so years. To keep up with his bills, he got a part time job in addition to working his full time job as a wine salesman, opened bank accounts in his own name and sold his house within six months of his divorce.

"Even prior to the divorce agreement, make sure you get your house court-ordered to be sold as soon as possible at fair market value," he says. "It means that your ex-wife has to move into different quarters. She'll do it with a pocket full of money and her own possessions."

Looking back, Peter says he learned many lessons during his divorce - some the hard way - and offers these tips so other men don't make similar mistakes:

- *Rent a PO Box, then ask your local post office to forward your mail to this new address.*
- *Call all of your creditors to change your billing address to your PO Box so that you receive all bills. Don't count on your wife to forward your mail.*
- *Pay alimony or child support by check. Each week, Peter sent his ex-wife a $125 check – certified return receipt - for groceries, gas and other routine expenses for her and their two young children.*
- *Hire an experienced divorce attorney. Peter says his attorney was neither experienced nor ethical and seemed more interested in aggravating his situation to rack up additional legal expenses than in helping him reach a quick and fair settlement.*

Back then, Peter requested custody of his children. His wife's escalating alcohol and prescription drug abuse and potentially physically abusive live-in boyfriend raised serious red flags. He even visited the local police station on two occasions because he firmly believed his children were in danger. However, the police officers claimed their hands were tied. At the time, he says everyone from the judges to child welfare workers were pro-mother.

"I must have seemed like a hysterical, maladjusted, ex-husband," says Peter, now 56 years-old and a member of M3.

Since no one outside his family would help, he turned inward. He told his children he would keep a close eye on them and encouraged them to speak about their concerns during their visits. Then one day, his ex-wife showed up three days late to pick up the children from his house. She later explained to a judge that she lost track of time while on a sailboat with her new boyfriend. The court finally acted, awarding Peter part-time custody. The children lived with him during the summer months and the rest of the year with their mother. But seven years after the divorce, he says both of his children, who were then 16 and 11, began living with him year-round.

In the long run, Peter believes it never pays to fight a divorce. Why would you want to be with someone who no longer loves or respects you, may be having affairs or constantly argues with you? Not to mention the thousands of dollars you'll spend on legal expenses.

"Get it done with," he says. "Come away with as much of yourself as you came into it with. Preserve as much as you can."

Alternative Paths

There are several different ways to obtain a divorce and settle your financial affairs: mediation, collaborative law (CL), arbitration and litigation.

In the past, people hired a divorce lawyer to litigate or present their case before a family court judge. While this traditional route still exists, consider mediation first because it's the least expensive, the quickest approach, solicits your input and give both sides the opportunity to reach a fair agreement. But if mediation doesn't work, try CL next. If you still can't reach agreement, explore litigation. Arbitration should be your last resort since it's typically used to address discreet issues.

Here are the potential benefits and downsides of each approach:

Mediation

Many people prefer mediation where they hire a mediator or third party to settle their disputes. They make their own decisions after working with each other toward a shared outcome.

In some states, anyone can hang a shingle as a mediator while in others, such as Maryland, mediators must complete a special training course to be court appointed, says Robert L. Baum, an attorney at the Law & Dispute Resolution Office of Robert L. Baum in Rockville, Md.

Mediation can be a small fraction of the cost of litigation. It's most effective when both parties can still talk to, not scream at, each other and essentially "be on the same intellectual page," says Baum. Although it may not be necessary, you can still bring your own attorney with you to each session.

"The role of a mediator is to be a facilitator of dialogue between the parties," says Baum, adding that mediators don't replace attorneys or give legal advice. "Mediators are never decision-makers for the parties."

As a mediator, Baum schedules three, three-hour sessions with clients who are going through the divorce process. One focuses on child custody, the second on financial issues and the last session on property. However, other mediators may only schedule two sessions. Either way, try to work out as much of the arrangements or details before the first session. He recalls one husband and wife who worked out almost every detail, drastically cutting their legal expenses. The mediation only lasted 45 minutes. Yet, another couple who couldn't agree on anything, required at least 10 sessions.

Mediation is only binding when both parties sign an agreement consenting to specific terms. That agreement becomes a binding contract, then later their divorce decree.

But if an agreement can't be reached and the couple ends up in court, he said anything said during the mediation is confidential. The mediator cannot be called as a witness to testify against one part or the other.

Collaborative Law (CL)

CL is a relatively new style of conflict resolution for divorce cases. Under this scenario, both parties agree to hire their own legal counsel to settle their case.

"The theory behind it is 95 to 97 percent of divorce cases are going to settle anyway so why hire Rambo who's going to destroy everything in their way and cost thousands and thousands of dollars when the case is going to be settled anyway," Baum says. "Start with something more logical and where you're going to end up, which is trying to settle the case."

If you choose this option, you and your wife must sign an agreement that your lawyers will not take your case to court. If negotiations break down, you'll have to choose new attorneys.

Like mediation, Baum says CL can be significantly less than litigation, or in some cases, just as much depending on how well each side compromises.

The cost of going to court can easily soar to tens of thousands of dollars, he says. With CL, you are responsible for paying all legal expenses as well as fees for financial planners and mental health professionals called divorce coaches who are also brought in to help you through the struggle of divorce.

One of the goals of divorce coaches, whose hourly fees typically start at $100, is to prevent emotional issues from entering negotiations.

"If a husband and wife want to beat themselves up over something that happened in the past or something that really irritated them, let them do that away from the lawyers who are charging hundreds of dollars each hour," explains Baum, adding that some CL lawyers won't accept your case unless you agree to hire divorce coaches. "It makes our discussions much more business-like."

There are many advantages of CL. For example, your lawyer is always by your side and each party has the right to examine any document presented during the negotiations. What's more, each lawyer pledges to do what's best for the interest of both parties and not take advantage of mistakes made by each other.

Litigation

If you've tried mediation and CL but still can't agree, then litigation is the next step. You and your wife each hire an attorney who represents your side in court. Besides paying huge expenses, there's another downside to this approach. Baum says children always feel the negative impact of litigation so try to avoid stepping into a courtroom. The end result may not be worth the emotional toll it takes on them and you.

Arbitration

People seeking this legal avenue are typically interested in one thing: quickly resolving a single aspect of their divorce that is private or confidential. Nothing that's addressed or filed becomes public. They hire a private arbitrator who listens to both parties and their witnesses, then makes a decision.

There are two types of arbitration - binding and nonbinding. In binding arbitration, the arbitrator's decision is the same as a judge's decision. However, your appeal rights are very limited, even more so than if you had a regular court hearing, says Baum.

Only certain issues can be resolved through binging arbitration, which varies from state to state. In Maryland, for instance, arbitrators can only address property issues.

But nonbinding arbitration is a different story. Also referred to as neutral fact finding, you and your wife would each present your case, then the arbitrator renders his or her findings or recommendations. Unlike binding arbitration, you each have the option of accepting or rejecting them. If accepted, you both sign an agreement, which then becomes binding.

Regardless of which approach appeals to you, always consult an experienced divorce lawyer before doing anything. Learn what rights you have and develop a good game plan before you enter the lion's den.

Home, Sweet Home

Oftentimes, men are the ones to move out of the house when a divorce is imminent. Big mistake, especially if you have children.

Although every case is different, leaving your home before your divorce is settled will influence a judge's decision when it comes to property settlement, visitation rights or joint custody of your children, says Randy Kessler, a divorce attorney at Kessler, Schwarz & Solomiany law firm in Atlanta.

"A house is an ambiguous asset, as opposed to cash," he explains. "If a guy leaves, gets to court, then the judge has to decide who gets the house, it's a lot easier for the judge to leave the house to the person who's already [living] there."

But if you stay put - even if that means sleeping in the basement or on the family room couch - and the judge still kicks you out, Kessler says it will probably work to your advantage down the road. The judge – who may feel a bit remorseful about uprooting you from the only home you've ever known in 10 or 20 years – may compensate you for something else like honoring your request for lower alimony payments, for example.

This same strategy can also be used as a psychological leverage. Some women place undue value on their home, says Kessler. For example, let's say you have $150,000 equity in your home and $100,000 in a joint savings account. If your wife really wants you to move out quickly, she may make a deal you can't refuse, such as leaving you the savings account in exchange for the house and no alimony payments.

"There's a psychological leverage you have when someone wants you out of the house," he says. "Your wife may forfeit valuable rights, assets or bargaining power. You lose that leverage if you leave the house before the negotiation."

Likewise, the longer the marriage, the more likely that the judge will give everybody a fair shake, even if it means your wife ends up paying you alimony and child support. The judge will consider what you forfeited to be married.

For instance, think about your relationship before you were married. Maybe your future wife lived in another state. You left school or a good paying job to be with her, then married her. Since then, her paychecks have been much bigger than yours. Or, maybe you stayed home with your young children. What did you sacrifice? If you can prove that you helped advance her career by abandoning your own, then the judge may award you alimony.

Judges usually care more about what happened yesterday, last week or last month than 10 years ago, adds Kessler. Being a drug addict seven years ago will be less important than if you've been clean for the past several years. Or if you had multiple affairs eight years ago but have been faithful for the last five years, the judge will focus on the latter. It shows you've struggled with issues and overcame them. That's why you need to be on your best behavior during a divorce. According to the judge, how you act today is often the best indicator of how you will act tomorrow.

But even if you mind your manners, you could still land in trouble. Sometimes, soon-to-be ex-wives can be very vindictive and resort to playing dirty. They may claim you physically abused them even if you never laid a hand on them. In such cases, they can immediately obtain a restraining order against you, which means you're forced out of your own home even though you did nothing wrong, says Kessler.

If you mildly suspect that your wife may be vengeful and act out in some way that could hurt you during your divorce, avoid falling in her trap. Do your best not to be provoked. Although your emotions are heightened and tensions may run high, never touch her. Never threaten her. Walk away instead of screaming or yelling. And whenever possible, never be alone with her. Leave the house if you have to or invite a friend or relative to stay with you. Hire a nanny who can be an objective witness. Find different ways to protect or insulate yourself. Just remember, your wife can lie, she can even hit herself on the head with a frying pan, but ultimately, she has the burden of proof.

Fortunately, false claims of abuse are not rampant. Still, you should act as if the judge is walking next to you wherever you go and that whatever you do or say will be featured on the front page of the local newspaper.

That's why it's a good idea to either contribute to or pay for your wife's divorce attorney. Besides being the ethical thing to do because it ensures fair representation, it can also help you score big points with the judge.

By doing so, Kessler says it makes you look like the good guy. If you end up in court, he says there's nothing better your attorney would like to do than inform the judge about how responsible you are like writing your wife's lawyer a check. That makes a favorable impression upon a judge. In some cases, he says the judge may even deduct that expense from her settlement.

Bottom line: Just think about every aspect of your divorce from the perspective of a trial judge. How would the judge like to see you behave? What could you say or do that would later prove embarrassing, childish or spiteful? Be prepared to be placed under the court's microscope and act accordingly.

Who Gets Custody?

Years ago, courts almost always ruled in favor of granting custody of children of tender years - those under the age of seven - to their mother. But times are changing. The cards are no longer stacked against men.

Most states now require family court to determine custody based on the best interest of the child, not the gender of the parent, says Michael Davidson, a divorce attorney at Davidson & Oeltgen law firm in Lexington, Ky.

"Most state statutes require equal consideration to be given to both parents," he says. "They're on an even playing field when they come to court nowadays as opposed to 20 or 30 years ago when it was just presumed [that children were better off with their mother]."

Davidson has seen more than his fair share of custody arrangements. He says the most innovative decision he ever heard was when the children remained in the house but every six months, the parents switched off living with them. Nowadays, more typical arrangements involve children visiting each parent, trading off weekends, holidays and maybe one evening each week between their mother and father.

To ensure a fair custody and visitation arrangement, Davidson offers these tips:

- Be flexible. Modify your work schedule to make yourself as accessible as possible to your children. It's unrealistic to expect your children to live with you if you work the midnight shift, unless your ex-wife is on the same schedule. Explore alternative work schedules with your boss. Maybe you can work from home, work four, 10-hour shifts or one week on, one week off. Otherwise, you may have to make a decision between your current job and spending more time with your children.

Instead of arguing with our ex-wife over the number of hours you can see your children each week, keep in mind that with school-age children, teachers are their primary caretakers. Many parents come home from work around six o'clock in the evening and spend no more than several hours with their children before they go to bed, then maybe another hour with them in the morning before they head off to school. And parents spend even less time with teenage children. "Flexibility is the key to the successful operation of joint custody," says Davidson.

- Play it smart. If your youngest child will soon turn 18 years of age, Davidson can't think of any compelling reason why you should file for divorce. Wait until the child's eighteenth birthday so you can avoid arguing about child custody and support. At that point, let your son or daughter decide his or her living arrangements.
- Maintain established routines. Children need stability, predictability and routines in their lives, which is what courts consider when awarding custody. The least disruption for your children, the better. For instance, if a nanny watches your children, the nanny should follow them from your ex-wife's house to your house during visitations. If they go to their grandparent's house every day after school, that routine should continue. Make sure your visitation or custody requests observe those existing routines whenever possible.
- Stay close. If you know you'll be the one to move out of the house, try to find a house or apartment that's close to your children's schools, especially if your kids don't drive. Also make sure that they each have a bed to sleep in when they visit. Your lawyer can then tell the judge —especially if you're asking for primary residential care - that your children will still be living in the same neighborhood, can socialize with the same friends, walk to and from school and sleep in their own bed.

  However, if you decide to move out of state - perhaps you've accepted a new job that's too good to turn down – it can create some problematic issues for the court involving the jurisdiction of custody. Make sure your attorney is very well versed in the Uniform Child Custody Jurisdiction and Enforcement Act (UCCJEA).

- Don't move out until your divorce is granted. While mentioned earlier, this bears repeating. "Once that damage is done, it's real hard to put the toothpaste back in the tube," says Davidson. "I've told my clients that if they're smart, they'll get back into that house before they file. They need to recognize going into the courtroom, that they already made a pretty bad mistake they might have to live with." He explains that the judge will feel they left their children and grant primary residential care to their wife.

  Staying in the house is especially important if the wife is excessively drinking, taking illegal drugs, physically abusive or showing signs of mental illness. If the father moves out before the case is resolved, Davidson says it's analogous to leaving his children in a burning automobile. The father can also be brought up on charges of abuse or dependency neglect for leaving his children in a dangerous environment.

  Sometimes, therapists who have been previously treating the wife can demonstrate why the children may be better off living with their father. Davidson says the court considers the mental and physical health of both parents before making a custodial decision. Your lawyer —as well as your ex wife's - can also request a mental health evaluation.

- Respect and honor your kids. Whenever you do spend time with your children, pick them up on time, don't make excuses for being late and never - ever — not show without calling with a reasonable explanation. Davidson says one of the biggest problems he sees is men placing their own needs in front of their children's needs. All your ex-wife has to do is tell a family court judge about your behavior. Imagine if you were the judge listening to this story:

  o   "He asked for all of this extra time with our kids, never spends it with them and is always late when he does show up," she says. "It's so upsetting to them. He gets their hopes up - daddy's gonna take us to the zoo - and he doesn't even have the courtesy to call to tell them he's not coming. You should see their face, judge, when they're sitting on the porch crying, wondering why their daddy doesn't love them."

Your credibility with the judge just plummeted to zero. Davidson says the judge could restrict, supervise, or even stop your visitations altogether if it's detrimental to your children or causes them to have a meltdown.

He explains that most, if not all, judges prefer not to deal with setting up visitation rights, let alone monitoring either parent's behavior. When recently researching standard visitation guidelines across the country, Davidson discovered that most guidelines were put into place by default. Judges actually want parents to come up with their own arrangements or they will decide for them. So try to work out a visitation schedule that is good for both you and your wife. Expect to compromise. Count on giving in a little, maybe a lot. Otherwise, you might get stuck with a visitation schedule that was far worse than what you originally planned.

If you need help developing a visitation schedule, ask the court to assign a parent coordinator, who is a mental health professional specifically involved in domestic family law. Coordinators help parents put aside their grudges and any "get even" mentality to make joint decisions that are based on what's best for their children.

Their hourly fee typically starts at $100. Still, they're well worth it, says Davidson. Instead of a judge calling the shots, you get to be involved in making decisions that will affect your future relationship with your children. He believes going into a courtroom and allowing a judge to decide your fate is synonymous with visiting an emergency room. You'll get immediate attention but won't feel well once you leave. But parent coordinators are like the family doctor you've known for years. They'll spend as much time as you need to resolve personal issues, then develop a plan that best addresses your individual circumstances.

Jeff

Jeff made the mistake of moving out of his house before his divorce was settled in 2001. Married for almost 20 years with three children, he says his wife's behavior changed. As a stay-at-home mom, she was spending money faster than he could make it, was no longer supportive of him and at least on one occasion, was physically abusive to their teenage son.

The constant arguing, endless confrontations and her reluctance to participate in marriage counseling were more than he could bear. He moved out before consulting an attorney. But when he met a divorce attorney at a men's support group coordinated by Men Mentoring Men, he was told to move back into his house. Although his wife no longer wanted him, he still moved back, agreeing to sleep in the basement.

There was virtually no communication between them, which made their divorce bitter. One of the decisions he now regrets is moving 45 minutes away, then later 90 minutes away from his children.

"I should have stayed closer in town," he says. Although his children were good students and, for the most part, well behaved, he couldn't do simple things for them like offer rides when needed or help them with their homework. Likewise, as his children grew older, the long distance became even more of a hurdle when planning visitations.

Eight years after his divorce, he lives in town with his girlfriend and his two children, now 17 and 19, who chose to live with them. His middle son lives away at college. The tables have since turned. His wife is now paying him child support.

Looking back, he says he would have done some things differently.

"My attorney advised me to fight for custody," says Jeff, who at the time, didn't think it was a good idea because of his traditional work schedule and the fact that his children would have to make new friends and attend different schools.

But he realizes that if he lived closer, they could have lived with him, which would have strengthened their relationship and helped ease the financial burden of supporting two households.

"Living physically closer is always on my mind," says Jeff, now 53 years-old and a member of M3. "I hear a lot about that from my [oldest] son who says I was never around. He felt deserted while in high school. I'm working on repairing that feeling but I don't think it will go away altogether."

Additional Thoughts:

1. "You don't know a woman 'til you've met her in court." –Norman Mailer, an American novelist, journalist, screenwriter and film director.

2. "Ah yes, divorce…from the Latin word meaning to rip out a man's genitals through his wallet." Comedian/Actor Robin Williams

3. "She cried and the judge wiped her tears with my checkbook." Tommy Manville, Manhattan socialite who was married 13 times to 11 women.

4. The average cost of a divorce in the US runs between $20,000 and $30,000.

5. One-third of married Americans have considered the idea of divorce.

6. Thirty six percent of divorced Americans claim verbal or physical abuse as the main cause of their divorce.

7. Men are more than twice as likely as women to cite sexual incompatibility as the cause for their failed marriage.

8. Women are more than twice as likely as men to divorce because of verbal or physical abuse.

9. Other causes of divorce: money (22%); someone new (18%); childrearing disagreements (13%); boredom (12%).

Middle Ground

There is a lawsuit called separate maintenance - which may be called by different names in other states - that enables people to receive the benefits of divorce without actually getting one. You can still establish custody, visitation rights and spousal support, live in separate houses or divvy up your financial assets, explains Randy Kessler at Kessler, Schwarz & Solomiany. Although infrequently used, he says people file for this suit if they're religiously opposed to a divorce, afraid or not yet ready to end their marriage.

Did You Know…

In most states, there's no such thing as a legal separation, says Randy Kessler at Kessler, Schwarz & Solomiany. When you file for divorce, it's apparent. But in a handful of states, such as Georgia, when filing for divorce, you must tell the court that you and your wife consider yourself legally separated or are in a bonafide state of separation, which means you're not having sex. Otherwise, he says your divorce can't be granted.

Resources:

International Academy of Collaborative Professionals
A global community of legal, mental health and financial professionals who work together to create client-centered processes for resolving conflict.
www.collaborativepractice.com

Association of Divorce Financial Planners
A group of financial planners who are trained and experienced in researching and analyzing personal, business and tax issues related to divorce. They help people achieve fair and workable agreements.
www.divorceandfinance.org

Directory of Divorce Mediators
A listing of divorce mediators in every state.
www.divorcehq.com/mediatordir.shtml

www.divorcesource.com
State listings of divorce-related professionals and information.

www.divorcesupport.com
Provides divorce information on family law topics, such as divorce, child custody, visitation, child support, alimony and property division.

http://family-law.freeadvice.com/child_custody/
The website answers frequently-asked questions about a wide variety of child custody issues.

www.greatdivorceadvice.com
This website offers a variety of information and resources ranging from advice on divorce tactics and father's rights to divorce-related books and a blog.

www.expertlaw.com
Provides legal help, information and resources.

www.fatherscustody.org
A national nonprofit organization dedicated to helping actively involved fathers gain custody of their children or pay reasonable child support based upon their current income and other factors

CHAPTER 3 ~

Making It Work

"**Y**A KNOW SOMETHING? You're a real jerk. That's just like you to be so selfish and immature. You haven't changed one bit. You only think about yourself and don't care about anyone else..."
Sound familiar? If you've been divorced for a while, chances are you've already had multiple conversations that started off this way. If you're newly divorced, don't be surprised if your ex-wife rattles off similar statements full of blame and hostility.

Just when you think the worst is over, your ex-wife declares war on you. You can't seem to say or do anything right. She screams at you because you were 10 minutes late picking up the kids. She writes a nasty email because you don't agree on something. Or she chews you out for letting your six year-old daughter stay up an extra 30 minutes on a school night.

More often than not, communicating with your ex-wife is going to be difficult at best. Even with a detailed custody agreement that covers every imaginable scenario, your conversations may still be strained. You may scream back, email an even nastier message or let your attorney do the talking. You've tried almost everything you know and nothing seems to work. You simply can't agree on anything, no matter how big or small the problem.

There's no need to raise the white flag. Surrendering is not an option. There are many different strategies or techniques you can implement that will offer positive results. While you may be unfamiliar with some of these practices, they all require you to put your ego aside. Remember, this isn't about what's best for you. It's all about what's best for your children. As the old saying goes, marriage is about the husband and wife. Divorce is about the children.

Your first step in establishing effective communication is realizing that repeatedly going to court or filing motions against your ex-wife only produces two outcomes: expensive legal fees and more anger or animosity between you. Conflict, especially when it involves a courtroom, pushes people apart. The more conflict, the greater the communication gap, says Nora Kalb Bushfield, an attorney in Atlanta and parenting coordinator (PC) who has handled divorce cases for the past 25 years.

"When you go into litigation, the court and attorneys tend to be in control," she says, explaining that divorce is 80 percent emotion. "As the situation escalates and communication breaks down between you and your spouse, other people step in. They say, "I know better, you don't know what you're doing so let me do it for you.""

In reality, she says you need to talk directly to your ex-wife, not your attorney. Take back that control. Don't give any attorney that power unless it's absolutely necessary. This not only enables you to settle current disputes like two mature adults, but also offers opportunities to learn and develop effective communication skills to resolve other issues through the years.

Besides, she says by continually filing motions because you can't figure out how to compromise or get along with each other just irritates judges. Some believe you're abusing the court or using the court inappropriately, which may land you in trouble.

Kalb Bushfield tells the story of a divorce case that happened several years ago. Instead of trying to find ways to communicate with each other about how to raise their eight-year-old son, the mother and father kept filing motions against each other for "ridiculous" things, she says, citing picking up the son five minutes late as an example. The couple ended up in court five times. The last time was at nine-thirty in the evening. Far from pleased, the judge tried a rather extreme tactic. He had both parents arrested for violating a child visitation provision. The mother - Kalb Bushfield's client - stayed in jail overnight before being released.

Apparently, spending a night in jail was a temporary fix. The couple managed to stay out of court for at least one year. Both had remarried and each had another baby. But when the father moved to another county, he retained another attorney who had to deal with a whole new set of judges. The endless motions or cross contempt actions were about to start all over again.

"We were ready to throw our hands up," she recalls.

This time around, however, Kalb Bushfield and the new attorney persuaded the couple to hire a PC, who teaches ex-spouses how to communicate with each other for the sake of their children. (More about PCs later). The counseling was so successful that the two families began celebrating family events together and have never returned to court.

While socializing with your ex-wife and her family may not be in your crystal ball, you can still learn how to maintain control when conversing with her. Kalb Bushfield, who also has a master's in social work degree, suggests tattooing these four words to your wrist so you never forget to use them: I understand, But, So.

The "I understand" part lets your ex-wife know that you understand her reasons. The "But" part allows you to express your feelings. The "So" portion is your suggested resolution.

Here's how using those words can work to your advantage: Let's say your wife becomes angry because you allowed your young daughter to go to sleep 30 minutes after her scheduled bedtime. Instead of verbally retaliating, consider saying something like, "I <u>understand</u> that Jessica has a schedule and needs at least eight hours of sleep. <u>But</u> we're now divorced, living apart and have different lifestyles along with different house rules. <u>So</u> let's see if we can come up with a compromise and try to get on the same page. What do you think about a bedtime range, between eight o'clock and eight-thirty?"

"If you don't recognize your ex-wife's position, she'll shut down and won't hear what you want to get to, which is the 'So'," she says. "It feels more like a command."

You may need to repeat the "I understand" process several times until you understand your wife's objection. Dig a little deeper each time. Keep going until she acknowledges that you've identified the real problem.

This technique will help you change the way you respond to your ex-wife, which will hopefully change the way she responds to you. That's the goal – to develop and use effective communication skills. But you may have to make the first move.

Develop Ground Rules

How do you and your ex-wife communicate with each other? Can either of you say anything you want no matter how unfair or hurtful it may be? Not a good idea, especially if your children are still young.

Create a set of rules that you both can live with and follow when communicating with each other about your children or making joint decisions. One rule at the top of your list should be to listen to each other without interrupting, says Wendy Davenson, a PC and licensed marriage and family therapist in Sandy Hook, Ct.

But that's hard to do because men and women often don't speak the same language, she says.

"Men speak in what is called report talk," she says, explaining that since they like to solve problems, they report what happened and how it happened, often without any emotion.

However, women speak in rapport talk, looking to be expressive. Considering this gap, one of the things men can do to enhance communication is to solicit input from their ex-wife when trying to fix or solve problems. Learn to say, "Here's an option. Would you like to hear it?"

Davenson says many women feel that they're coerced into decisions because their ex-husbands control their income. Whether you do or not, try a collaborative approach instead, which validates your ex-wife's perspective. For instance, consider using phrases like: "You know what, you've got a really good point. How about if we....", or "Gee, I never thought of it from that perspective, that's a really good idea...".

This approach demonstrates that you're listening to her ideas, considering her suggestions and involving her in the decision-making process. No one – man or woman - likes to have decisions crammed down his or her throat. So how do you come across? Are you a good listener? Are you accepting of her ideas? Or, are your opinions and ideas the only ones that matter?

Davenson offers 10 more rules:

- Avoid name-calling, killer statements or put-downs. Insults will just create more tension or animosity between you and your ex.
- Meet in a public place like a coffee shop. You can come better prepared and will be less inclined to scream at each other when trying to resolve issues. An alternative is to email each other once a week with a list of questions or concerns that came up about your children during the week. This way, both parents are always kept in the loop.
- Steer clear from history lessons. Bringing up the past should be taboo as well as making statements like, "You always do that".
- Place a photo of your children on the table during your conversations, or if emailing, next to your computer. This will help you stay focused on the task at hand, which is doing what's best for your children.
- Email your concerns in advance of each meeting so both of you have a chance to think them through. If you call your ex-wife and spring a problem on her without any warning, then insist upon your solution, Davenson says don't be surprised if she becomes resentful.

- Stay on topic. Focus on one problem at a time, not what may happen weeks or months from now.
- Create an agenda. Decide what issues to address before your meeting and possibly agree on a time frame for each issue.
- Be flexible. Put your ego aside and listen - really listen - to each other's ideas.
- Brainstorm solutions. Your ex-wife wants Tommy to go to a private school but you favor public school. Instead of arguing about it, explore options. Maybe there's another school or even summer program that's less expensive and offers some of the same courses or benefits of the private school.
- Focus on what's best for your children instead of searching for ways to get revenge for the wrongs you feel have been done to you.

One of the most difficult rules to follow for either parent is to stop saying, 'I know what's best for my children," says Davenson, adding that the younger the child, the more protective the mother is and less confidant that the father can do basic things like change diapers or bottle-feed. If your ex-wife makes this statement, then digs in her heels, sometimes it's best to walk way. She may not budge, even if you mention more reasonable or realistic alternatives. This may also be her attempt to control the situation or perhaps control you. Come back to the issue later, says Davenson, when both of you have had ample time to step back and re-evaluate your options.

Events, celebrations and holidays can also trigger trouble. Your ex-wife may not invite you to your four year-old son's birthday party. While you may be angry, thinking it's unfair, consider your son. When you and your ex-wife are together in the same room, is there any tension or hostility? Do you always argue, even about insignificant things? If yes, then for the sake of your son, it's best to stay away.

Davenson recommends that each parent alternate years. The father hosts a party for his son and son's friends during the odd years, and the mother during the even years. During off years, each parent only needs to hold a small family gathering, inviting grandparents or aunts and uncles. Just don't compete by hosting a separate party for your son and his friends during the same year.

"Kids end up getting greedy, getting four parties each year," she says. "Parents have guilt from divorcing to begin with so they end up spoiling the kids to make themselves feel better. That's not good for the kids."

Another common problem: Oftentimes, Davenson says some husbands expect their ex-wife to make them copies of their children's soccer schedule, report cards, medical records and other documents. Expectations like these may only lead to more anger and frustration. It's best to ask the school to mail you a copy of your daughter's report card. Talk to your son's coach about the soccer schedule. Request copies of their medical forms or records from their pediatrician. Specify in your divorce agreement that the schools your children attend must send information to both you and your ex.

But a much easier way is for both of you to post information about your children on online calendars that are password protected. You'll each know when Michelle is playing soccer or David has a doctor's appointment (see resource section at the end of this chapter for websites that offer online schedules.)

There will also be times when you must make important decisions— anything from your child needing braces to surgery. If your ex-wife is reluctant to share information with you or may not be able to address all of our questions, call the orthodontist or doctor for an appointment. Invite your ex-wife to come along. She may turn you down but at least you offered an olive branch, something she may later appreciate.

Unfortunately, you'll probably make split-second decisions as well. If your daughter is seriously injured while playing sports, for instance, or in a car accident, she may need immediate surgery. When notifying your ex-wife, be careful how you describe the scenario. Consider the two statements below:

"Jessica hurt her leg playing soccer. She's at the hospital. The doctor mentioned different things we can do. I decided surgery was the best way to go so she's being operated on right now."

--or—

"Jessica hurt her leg playing soccer. She's at the hospital. The doctor mentioned different things we can do but recommended surgery so she's being operated on right now.

Hear, or better yet, feel the difference? Although both statements are accurate, the last one takes the heat off you. Davenson says ex-wives get ticked off when they feel there was a unilateral decision made without their consultation. If you use the second statement, she can't legitimately complain that you followed the doctor's advice.

Helping Hands

Sometimes, no matter how hard you try, your ex-wife won't behave in a civil manner. She may still be very hurt and angry about your divorce. So she refuses to return your calls or emails, shares absolutely zero information with you about your children, is highly disrespectful toward you in front of your children, makes immediate, unrealistic demands regarding your children or consistently screams at you. The communication between you two has collapsed.

It's the time to call in the Calvary.

There are actually five types of professionals whom can help you establish communication between you and your ex-wife or get it back on track, says Susan Boyan, a PC, licensed marriage and family therapist and co-founder of the Cooperative Parenting Institute (www.cooperativeparenting.com).

You and your ex-wife can either sign a stipulation agreeing to external help or your attorney can request that the judge appoint an outside person, even without your wife's consent. Keep in mind that no matter what the scenario is or which professional you choose, you and your ex-wife will pay the bill for the individual's services, which can amount to thousands of dollars each.

Guardians ad Litem are attorneys appointed by the court. They represent and protect your children. They'll investigate what both parents say about each other, meet with you, your ex-wife and your children, then make a recommendation to the court.

"Guardians have a lot of leverage with the courts," Boyan says, adding that this approach can be risky because some guardians may be biased or not well trained in psychology and unable to spot problems, such as if your ex-wife tries to alienate you from your children or is emotionally unstable. However, she says guardians are effective at recognizing overt problems like your ex-wife's abuse of drugs or alcohol or neglect of your children.

Custody Evaluators are generally psychologists or mental health professionals who collect data and also perform a series of psychological tests on you and your ex-wife. Evaluators are generally better equipped to deal with the subtleties of manipulation, emotional instability and can recognize alienation issues. They meet with each member of your immediate family, then write a report to the court. While the courts do lean heavily on their findings, Boyan says these individuals tend to cost more than the other four professionals.

Late Case Evaluators listen to both you and your ex-wife, just like a judge. Based on the data collected, they make hypothetical decisions or rulings. "If I were the judge, I would rule this way…" Consider this a trial run, which gives parents an idea as to where they would stand and helps them decide whether or not to pursue litigation.

Mediators (who are also mentioned in chapter two) are sometimes used as a last ditch effort before going to court. They don't offer opinions but give both mom and dad an opportunity to jointly make key decisions regarding their children. When parents are directly involved in the decision-making process, they're more apt to follow through and observe whatever guidelines or rules they establish. Since this is a confidential process, mediators can't testify on behalf of one parent or the other. While this process is easy on the kids, Boyan says it works well with mild conflict divorces, not high conflict or problematic cases.

Parenting Coordinators are ideal for high conflict divorce cases. Most PCs are therapists or other mental health professionals who, unlike mediators, reveal their observations in court. However, most don't write reports. Instead, they work with both parents in the same room at the same time and, over a short period of time, receive a very accurate view of the dynamics between the ex-spouses. They give opinions, except on custody. But they can make statements to the judge, such as, "If this custody arrangement continues, the children are going to have this problem," which Boyan says usually spells a custody change.

"It's much more direct than therapy," says Boyan. "One judge called it the two-by-four approach."

Most PCs also videotape their sessions because they're so high conflict. Some tapes actually make their way into the courtroom. This is a distinct advantage over the other approaches since a video can reveal what guardians, custody evaluators or psychological tests may have missed. After watching a video, judges better understand how parents act and can even overturn previous rulings.

That happened in the case of one father who returned to court several times, requesting custody of his nine year-old daughter because he believed her mother was emotionally unstable, recalls Boyan. At first, the judge appointed a guardian, who reached the same conclusion as the father. But the judge disagreed. Then a therapist counseled the young girl and reached the same decision. The same judge still wouldn't budge, claiming the therapist was biased. On the third try, thousands of dollars later, the dad's attorney requested a PC, who was Boyan.

"The mom was very disturbed," says Boyan. "Now I come in with a videotape of a sample session and testify to the kinds of things this woman was doing and how dangerous it was for the little girl to remain with her. The same judge finally got it. Dad got custody. Mom had supervised visits. There's nothing like having a videotape or DVD that speaks."

She says PCs do well in getting parents to cooperate with each other partly because they hold them accountable for their actions. Consider a mom who refuses to release her children to their father for the weekend. The PC is "going to be all over her behind", says Boyan, sending both attorneys a memo about how she violated her custody agreement.

Ideally, Boyan suggests that fathers in high conflict divorces ask the judge to appoint a PC as part of his settlement agreement. If that's not possible, then use a PC as leverage. For example, maybe your ex-wife wants to spend Christmas this year with your children even though it's your turn. Tell her you'll agree if she agrees in writing to work with a PC.

At the very least, ask her to meet with the PC. Sometimes, Boyan says ex-spouses who are unstable are so convinced that what they're doing is right that they end up wanting a PC, too. That actually occurred. Boyan set up a meeting with an ex-wife whose ex-spouse felt she was unstable. During the meeting, she talked about how he had harassed her and how terrible he treated her, which wasn't true. She felt as if she was the victim, not the other way around. By the end of the meeting, she insisted on using a PC, says Boyan.

Once an ex-wife signs the PC stipulation, she can't quit. If she refuses to cooperate, the ex-husband's attorney files a motion and the PC is subpoenaed, then testifies as to the mother's troubled behavior.

"If dad doesn't get custody but really wants it, get the judge to appoint a PC post the divorce decree," says Boyan. "I've seen custody switched because after working with a PC for a year, the truth comes out. The judge completely missed it. It's not over until the PC squeals."

If you decide to go the PC route, there are some things you need to consider. As a PC, licensed professional counselor and co-founder and director of the Cooperative Parenting Institute, Ann Marie Termini lays out strict boundaries from the start for her clients.

They can't contact her by phone or email, with the exception of cancelling or rescheduling appointments or to schedule an initial consult.

"Every communication needs to take place in the session with both parents present so I can be more objective and hear both views at one time," she says. "Understand that the PC is an advocate for your child, not for either one of the parents."

PCs also educate parents about how their divorce is affecting their children. At one point, she says one parent will think she is biased because she is favoring the other parent. Then a month or so later, they trade places. She says it's not unusual for PCs to be considered biased whenever one parent thinks the other is getting his or her way.

The process is a learning curve for both the PC and parents. To a certain extent, PCs ask you to place your trust in them, which is often very hard to do, Termini says. Just make sure they're credible, trustworthy and ethical in their practices.

No matter whom you hire or what communication strategy you use, doing what's best for your children should always be your prime motivation behind each and every conversation with your ex-wife. Don't cross boundaries into each other's personal space, adds Termini. Likewise, don't pay too much attention to what your friends or family say because they may not be objective or understand your children's needs.

Termini suggests setting clear boundaries around the communication process. Make requests, not demands, and minimize conversations to the issue at heart.

"Very structured interactions will help you understand your own boundaries and not let you bleed into past marital issues," says Termini. "Focus on the present, focus on one problem versus the past and focus on your child."

Hard Lessons

Ed

When Ed divorced his ex-wife back in 1981, he focused on maintaining a great relationship with his one year-old son, who was living with his ex-wife.

"My priority was my relationship with my son," says Ed, a psychologist, artist and M3 member. "So all the communication I had with my ex-wife centered around maintaining a good relationship with her and anybody else she got involved with in order for me to stay in a good relationship with my son."

Even if he was angry at things she said or did, he rarely let on. To avoid constant bickering, he expressed his emotions to individuals in his support network who were objective and could view his circumstance from a distance. They felt comfortable saying either, "Ed, you're perfectly right, you need to pursue it," or "Ed, you're being a jerk, let it go."

But what helped Ed and his ex-wife start on the right communication path was divorce mediation, not litigation where attorneys often speak on your behalf. He says mediation helped set the stage for how they would communicate after their divorce. It taught them how to compromise, ignore the past and not let anger or other negative emotions influence their decisions concerning their son.

He says maintaining a relationship with his son was like the North Star, guiding all of his communications and actions. Besides, as a protective father, he knew problems between him and his ex-wife would ultimately trickle down to their son. "For a divorced or separated man, one of the best ways to protect their children is to keep them reasonably clear of the bullshit."

You should also extend that same philosophy to your ex-wife's boyfriends or new husband. Put any jealousy aside and develop a civil relationship with them.

"If the man is a good man, appreciate the fact that your child or children are around a good man, rather than an asshole," says Ed. "Remember that the happier your ex-wife is, the better off you are."

Still, Ed has one regret. Looking back, he's sorry he didn't show his ex-wife more appreciation along the way for being a good mother to their son and supporting Ed's desire to play a significant role in their son's life. He says some men have myopic vision, focusing only on their experiences, how they were wronged or what they missed out on.

"I should have seen it through her eyes and acknowledged it, and had more appreciation of what she was doing," he says, adding that years later, he did express his appreciation to her. She simply replied, "Thank you". But how she responded wasn't nearly as important as that it was said, he explains.

Ron

Ed may have been luckier than most divorcing husbands. Some ex-wives aren't the least bit supportive or cooperative. Ron, a salesman and M3 member, did whatever his ex-wife asked just to keep the peace. Divorced in 1997, his ex-wife had residential custody of their two young sons.

But his ex-wife, who had three other children with her first husband, wanted more freedom, he says. This was her second set of kids and she was tired of playing mother. So she increasingly placed more demands on Ron that were often unrealistic.

"She would call me and say, 'You've got to pick them up right now or I'm going to leave them on the doorstep,'" he recalls, adding that he lived 40 miles away. "So I kept assuming more responsibility. The guilt of divorce caused me to not set boundaries or say what is it I'm willing to do and where am I going to draw the line. Frankly, I was not standing up to what was important."

Not anymore. Ron changed his ways 18 months into his divorce after his ex-wife suddenly informed him that she sold her house, was moving to Las Vegas in 30 days and taking their children with her.

While she got away with using their children as leverage to get what she wanted, it wasn't going to work anymore.

Ron made sure of that. As an active father, he vehemently fought his ex-wife in court and was awarded custody of their two children. Then he drew lines in the sand.

She could only call him if there was an emergency. Communication would now be by email. Still, she tested his limits by sending seven or eight nasty emails each week, some even from her third husband. He says things got so nasty that they stopped communicating with each other for one year and worked through their attorneys. Now she sends three or four emails a month along with a phone call and text messages every now and then. Ron says he responds to all of her questions via email and also sends her a monthly update about their children. All emails are fact-based, short and to the point, he says.

He no longer caters to her whims. One year, the week before Thanksgiving, she asked him to send both children to her for a visit. He responded "no", calmly and coolly, reminding her that according to their custody agreement, she needs to notify him three months in advance with irregular visitation requests.

Among the biggest lessons Ron learned is not to take the bait. Realize that your ex-wife knows how to push all of your hot buttons to make you feel *angry or out of control. Don't allow yourself to be sucked into any mind games that distract you from important matters regarding your children.*

For example, if you know answering her phone call could result in a screaming match, don't take the call. Structure your conversations via email. If she still calls, politely hang up. But at the same time, don't alienate her. He says it's critical that both parents are supportive of each other and each have a say in their children's lives.

"Always keep the higher vision for yourself and your children in mind when dealing with communications," he says. "Prove to your kids that relationships aren't about people screaming and yelling or not getting along. It's so important to put stuff aside, never say a bad word about your ex and try to have an olive branch out there."

Consistency Matters

Young children typically require much more consistency when it comes to household rules.

Bruce Forman, Ph.D., psychologist and PC in Weston, Fla., says children usually under the age of nine need to follow one set of rules whether they're staying at either mom's or dad's house. Establishing consistent rules and daily routines are important for the healthy development of young children so both mom and dad need to work together to develop a list of rules they each agree to follow.

For example, jointly make rules about:

- Homework: When should your children complete their homework? After school or after dinner? Where can they finish their homework? In their room, in front of the TV or at a friend's house?
- Bedtime: What time should they go to bed on school days and on weekends? Can they sleep over at a friend's house on a school night?
- Dress: What kind of clothes can they wear to school? Can young girls wear makeup, short skirts or other popular, yet revealing, clothing to school?
- Communication: What kind of language are children allowed to

use? What type of standard punishment - if any – do they receive for using profanity or being disrespectful to either parent?

- Mealtime: When should they eat dinner? Can they eat in front of the TV? Can they answer their cell phone during dinner? Can they eat dessert if they don't finish their hamburger?
- What friends can they socialize with?

Forman says the more in sync parents are on such issues, the fewer arguments they'll have over raising their children. So will keeping a set of each child's clothes and other personal items at each household.

"I've seen situations where the mom would conveniently forget to pack clothes, underwear and socks," he says, adding that the father had to continually buy clothes for his children when they came to visit, which became very expensive. "He finally said to his kids, 'Leave them here. When you stay here, these are your clothes.'"

Divorce Rules

1. Do not talk badly about my other parent. (*This makes me feel torn apart! It also makes me feel bad about myself.*)

2. Do not talk about my other parent's friends or relatives. (*Let me care for someone even if you don't.*)

3. Do not talk about the divorce or other grown-up stuff. (*This makes me feel sick. Please leave me out of it.*)

4. Do not talk about child support. (*This makes me feel guilty or like I'm a possession instead of your kid.*)

5. Do not make me feel bad when I enjoy time with my other parent. (*This makes me afraid to tell you things.*)

6. Do not block my visits or prevent me from speaking to my other parent on the phone. (*This makes me very upset.*)

7. Do not interrupt my time with my other parent by calling too much or by planning my activities during our time together.

8. Do not argue in front of me or on the phone when I can hear you. (*This turns my stomach inside out!*)

9. Do not ask me to spy for you when I'm at my other parent's home. (*This makes me feel disloyal and dishonest.*)

10. Do not ask me to keep secrets from my other parent. (*Secrets make me feel anxious.*)

11. Do not ask me questions about my other parent's life. (*This makes me uncomfortable. Just let me tell you.*)

12. Do not give me verbal messages to deliver to my other parent. (*I end up feeling anxious about their reaction. Please call them, leave them a message at work or put a note in the mail.*)

13. Do not send written messages with me or place them in my bag. (*This also makes me uncomfortable.*)

14. Do not blame my other parent for the divorce or for things that go wrong in your life. (*This really feels terrible! I end up wanting to defend them from your attack. Sometimes it makes me feel sorry for you and want to protect you. I just want to be a kid, so please, please...stop putting me in the middle!*)

15. Do not treat me like an adult. (*It causes way too much stress for me.*) Please find a friend or therapist to talk with.

16. Do not ignore my other parent or sit on opposite sides of the room during my school or sports activities. (*This makes me feel sad and embarrassed. Please act like parents and be friendly, even if it is just for me.*)

17. Do let me take items to my other home as long as I can carry them back and forth. (*Otherwise it feels like you are treating me like a possession.*)

18. Do not use guilt to pressure me to love you more and do not ask me where I want to live.

19. Do realize that I have two homes, not just one. (*It doesn't matter how much time I spend there.*) I'd also really appreciate it if you would let my other parent come into our house every now and then, because it's my home too!

20. Do let me love both of you and see each of you as much as possible!

Thanks, your loving child XXXX OOOO

More tips:

1. Stay focused on your child's problem, not the problems you're having with your ex-wife.

2. Don't interrupt or get defensive.

3. Don't express your opinions as fact.

4. Lower your voice. More than likely, she will, too.

5. Avoid starting sentences with, "You always…" or "You never…"

6. Be flexible when trying to solve problems.

7. Don't write email messages in caps. It will seem like you're shouting.

8. Use "I" statements to express your feelings, such as, "I feel frustrated when you…."

Resources:

Parenting Coordination Central
www.parentingcoordinationcentral.com
Provides a state listing of parent coordinators, a joint custody checklist, information and resources.

American Association for American and Family Therapy
www.aamft.org
Offers a therapist locator for each state.

Youth Service Bureaus
(US Department of Health and Human Services, Administration for Children & Families)
www.acf.hhs.gov/programs/fysb/
Provides a wide range of comprehensive services at the local, state and national levels.

Separated Parenting Access & Resource Center (S.P.A.R.C.)
http://deltabravo.net
Offers useful information and tools for noncustodial parents.

Sharekids.com
www.Sharekids.com
A co-parenting system and online schedule designed to assist individuals in managing child-sharing between homes.

CustodyIQ.com
www.CustodyIQ.com
Offers information, resources and non-legal advice on joint custody issues to separating or divorcing parents.

Parentingtime.net
http://parentingtime.net
Offers OPTIMAL, an online custody calendar that allows parents to schedule and track parenting time and monitor compliance with their custody arrangement.

Don't forget to check with local religious organizations like Catholic Social Services or Jewish Social Service Agency that may offer counseling services.

CHAPTER 4 -
Disneyland Dad

T HE TIME HAS come for one of the most painful parts of divorce: Moving out. You've packed your bags and are leaving the safe and loving environment that what was once your home for a number of years. As you take one last look around the house, a flood of memories suddenly hit you. All the times you read your children a bedtime story. Those lively family dinners. Helping your kids do their homework. Playing soccer in the backyard. Making ice cream sundaes together.

Moving out is tough under any circumstance, even if your divorce is mutual. There are at least a million questions that cross your mind, yet no comforting answers. Can I still be a good father if I'm no longer living with them? How can I remain active in their lives? Will they hate me for moving out? Will they think I am abandoning them?

But fathers who have residential custody of their children fare no better. Hundreds of concerns and emotions overwhelm them, making them question their ability as a good parent. Can we adjust without their mother living here? Can I juggle working, shopping, chauffeuring, making dinner and cleaning the house? Will I know what to do when something goes wrong?

Whether living with their children or not, some fathers have found creative ways to develop strong relationships with their kids after divorce. Others have allowed their experience and pain to push them away.

Just like building any relationship, developing strong ties with you children requires love, energy and commitment. Being a good father is a full time job. There will be days when you wonder how you're going to survive past lunch. But all of your efforts and patience will generate huge rewards - lifelong, loving and trusting relationships with your children.

Reaching Out

How you communicate with your children will define the type of relationship you have with them, both today and in the future, says Jeanne Segal, Ph.D., a licensed child, marriage and family counselor in Santa Monica, Calif.

Don't limit your communication to phone talk or written messages via texting or email. Providing your ex spouse is supportive and doesn't try to sabotage your efforts, try something visual like routinely sending them pictures, drawings or cards, especially if they're young.

"Any kind of visual communication is important and makes kids feel safe and cared about, that somebody is looking after them," says Segal, who's also managing editor of www.helpguide.org and author of The Language of Emotional Intelligence. "That's what you want to give your kids - your loving, caring presence, whether you're there in the flesh or not."

It doesn't matter what photos you take or what the drawings resemble. For example, she says you can send a photo with the caption, "Here's a photo of me missing you." The secret of doing this well is having a real understanding of what makes your children laugh or happy. If your young daughter loves animals, for instance, then send her photos, cards or drawings of cute animals, which is a way you can continuously connect or bond with her as she grows.

You can also create pictures with words. When talking to your child on the phone, consider saying, "Picture that I'm now giving you a big hug and kiss. Can you feel it?" If your children are young—around the age of three or four – you can also ask them to draw their feelings about your divorce so you get a better sense of how they're coping with it. Segal says any time you can bring in sensory information, children will feel better emotionally.

With teenagers, you have more options. Keep in mind that the entry into their trust is listening, says Segal. If they're real angry with you, you may hear the resentment in their voice. Or they may pout during visitations. You can say things like, "I hear that (or see that). Do you want to tell me what that's all about?" Then sit back and listen. Really listen. Don't defend yourself, justify your actions, cut them short, or criticize them regardless of whether you think they're being fair or not.

"They'll come up with all kinds of things, especially if they're feeling bad," Segal says, adding that expressing such emotions are indeed flattering because they think they're losing someone they care about – you. "You just have to listen and be up for that. Once they trust you can do that, they're going to lighten up. That's what will help them feel less pissy."

Since your own life can be chaotic, it can be easy to forget the details of your children's every day life. Don't. Make a list if you have to. Your teenage son may confide in you that he's excited about taking a girl he really likes to a party Friday night. In his eyes, his date is just as important as the big client you've been trying to reel in for the past few months. If you forget to ask him how the date went, he may believe you don't care about him or aren't interested in his life any more.

But sometimes, no matter what you say to teenage children, it's always wrong or they jump to the wrong conclusion. So when they become angry, use humor, which diffuses conflict or tension. But be careful not to use sarcasm because it may make them feel as if you're laughing at them and make them even angrier.

What's important with children of any age is that you spend quality time with them. Establish an emotional connection. Forget buying them presents or taking them on expensive vacations. Instead, walk the dog together. Play ball in the park. Bake cookies. Read to them. Play a computer game. Go for ice cream. Segal says being a great dad—whether you're divorced or not - is all about the drive, not about the destination.

Pete

Since he was divorced in 2005, Pete found a unique way to spend quality time with his daughter, who's almost nine years-old today. As part of his divorce agreement, he meets his ex-wife and daughter at a specified mall, more than one hour away from his home. His ex-wife, who lives with their daughter in a neighboring state, goes off on her own, leaving their daughter with Pete from five-thirty in the afternoon until eight o'clock that evening, then drives their daughter back home.

The evening is divided into three parts: doing homework, eating and playing. Pete says sometimes they'll go bowling, watch a movie, go to an arcade or play air hockey.

"Usually, I like her to get her homework out of the way but sometimes she doesn't want to so I tell her it's your choice but we have to do homework," says Pete, a 54 year-old business development consultant. "That pulls her into the decision-making. She knows she made a decision and has to stick with it."

Over the past four years, Pete, who's a member of M3, has cancelled just a handful of these father-daughter dates due to business obligations. But he personally explains why, comparing it to things his daughter can relate to like the need to complete her homework or school projects on time or taking an important test in school. Then she understands, he says, adding that while she may be disappointed, she's never angry or thinks he doesn't love her anymore.

Pete also calls his daughter almost every night they're not together. While they have a close relationship, sometimes he'll kick-start conversations by asking her what's the funniest or best thing that happened to her that day. Then he responds to the same questions, which he says is a good way to connect to daily events in your children's lives.

Like most children, his daughter has definite ideas about how she wants to spend their weekends together and other times during the year. By jointly making these decisions, he knows she'll have fun, consider his home as a happy, safe place and perhaps best of all, spend time with someone she loves and adores - her daddy.

Plenty of Choices

While there are many creative and effective ways to interact with your children as a divorced dad, the context in which it's done is more important than what is being done, explains Lois Nightingale, Ph.D., a clinical psychologist in Yorba Linda, Calif.

As an example, consider a divorced dad who uses a notebook or journal for him and his son. Both can write anything they want that expresses their feelings toward each other or reminds them of each other while they're apart. The father could write something like, "I'm so proud of you for getting a B+ on that math test. I know how hard you studied for it. When I was your age, I remember...." The next time he sees his son, he hands him the journal. The son then takes some time to write his own passage regarding his father. Maybe it's about his favorite part of the weekend they just spent together. Then when they see each other again, the son hands back the journal to his father. The process keeps repeating itself.

But what would happen if the father consistently whines in the journal, complaining about how much he misses his son, how sad or lonely he feels and that he's not having fun anymore.

"That kind of emotion is very damaging to children," says Nightingale. "I see so many kids worried about the parent that they don't see often, worried that [he] is just miserable without them. Children get stomachaches, do terrible in school. [Dads] need to be positive, give lots of compliments, show that they're responsible for their own feelings and make sure their kids know they're having fun without them."

So pay attention to what you say to your children, which is more important than how or where your message is delivered.

Still, if you're looking for fun ways to emotionally connect with your kids as a divorced dad, consider these suggestions by Nightingale:

- Memory Box: During the times you and your children are apart, place things in a memory box that pertain to their interests. Nightingale tells the story of a father and son whose hobby was cars. When the son couldn't attend a car show with his father, the dad created a memory box of the show, which contained pictures of cool cars, the show's program, give-aways and other mementos he collected at the show. The dad gave his son the box and also told him lively stories about the show, creating a wonderful memory between them.

- Fairytales: When talking with young children on the phone, create a fairytale. You start the first sentence, they say the next, then keep alternating. "You get a lot of information about what goes on in a child's life if you can get them to do this back and forth fantasy," says Nightingale, adding that you can also weave in advice.

- Picture Perfect: If you and your children have computers equipped with cameras, consider using Skype, which is software that enables you to make free video phone calls over the Internet. You and your children can see each other as you talk.

- Conversation Starters: Young children have a hard time expressing how they feel. So the next time you call, ask them to say one thing they were happy about, one thing they were sad about and one thing they were proud of that day. Then you do the same. By sharing emotions, you not only teach your children a vocabulary of feelings, but also create an emotional safety net. For instance, your daughter may be sad because Billy picked on her today. Don't problem-solve by asking if she told her teacher or mother. Nightingale says the focus needs to be on sharing feelings. Instead ask questions like, "How do you still feel about that?" "How did you handle that?" or, "It sounds like you were really strong".

"A lot of dads shut children down by going for solutions," she says. "The more you can stay with the child's tension, the better your relationship is going to be with your children. You need to be strong enough to be there for them while they're sad today."

- **Missing Mom**: During a visitation, if your young daughter misses her mom, give her unlimited phone access to her mother. If it gets out-of-hand, like calling every 30 minutes, set some boundaries and involve your daughter in making something special for her mother, like a picture or card. Nightingale says this will give your daughter the emotional experience of feeling connected to your ex-wife. Besides, it also shows that you respect your child's feelings.

- **Healthy and Happy**: If your children live with your ex-wife, make sure they eat nutritious food and sleep the same amount of hours they normally do. Lack of sleep along with too much junk food can make them really hard to manage. Also, don't skip any hygiene habits like brushing their teeth, which can come back to haunt you.

- **Instant Recall:** Ask your children to write a journal about their day or weekend before leaving your home. Nightingale says children live very much in the moment. By drawing a picture or writing a story about their recent experiences, they can relive the fun or adventure.

- **Say Yes:** With teenagers, their friends are more important than their parents. If your teen wants to bring a friend along the next time you spend time together, say yes, whenever possible. Many teenagers stop seeing their father because he won't allow them to invite their friends.

- **Private Space:** Create a special place in your home for your child's belongings. Nightingale points to several divorced dads who each live in a motor home and designated a drawer just for their child. It tells children they're important and bonds them to you and your home.

- **Do As You Say:** If you tell your son you'll attend his soccer game, be there on time. If you tell your daughter you'll pick her up at nine o'clock to take her out to breakfast, follow through. If you're going to be late, call to explain why. Don't be known as the dad who always breaks his promises.

- **Changing Rules:** If your child wants to follow the rules observed at your ex-wife's house, not at your home, don't give in or you may soon regret it. Nightingale suggests saying, "Yes, mom does let you stay up until ten o'clock. But these are the rules at my house that I'm comfortable with." She says kids do understand that rules change in different environments. For example, they understand they have to raise their hand to talk in class but don't need to at the dinner table.

Whatever you do, just look at the bigger goal, which is creating memories, emotional safety and a lifetime relationship. Nightingale says dads can play a powerful role in the life of their children, even if they're miles away.

Just think about the most influential person in your life. Nightingale poses this question to some of her patients. Oftentimes, it's not their parents. Then she asks how much time they spent with this person.

"Just because you have less time with a child, doesn't mean you can't possibly be the most influential person in that kid's life," she says.

Growing Pains

While children respond differently to their parent's divorce, their age can sometimes help you gain insight into how they're feeling and predict their behavior. This can be a powerful tool for any father, especially long distance dads, who can be better prepared to help their kids accept their parents' divorce, move on with their life and, hopefully, be happy.

It's important to be sensitive to what your children are going through so you can develop a strong bond with them, says Sharona Stone, a licensed clinical social worker in Centennial, Co., who specializes in child development.

"Children who have parents who miss the emotional boat are more likely to be distant as teenagers and adults because the value of sharing experiences has not been developed," she explains, adding that a child's emotional responses to divorce can range from subdued reactions to mood fluctuations and dramatic mood swings. "Children are more cooperative when they believe their thoughts and feelings are important to a parent."

Consider how children in the following age groups may react to their parent's divorce in the months ahead:

Very young children (up to 18 or 24 months):

How they feel: Babies and toddlers may experience separation anxiety during the absence of their primary caretaker. Stone compares it to seeing only part of a picture when they're accustomed to seeing the whole screen. They can also pick up tension from you or your ex-wife while being held.

How they act: They may cry or scream more than usual and be more difficult to calm. That can lead to exhaustion, despair, apathy, loss of appetite and disrupted sleep or a desire to sleep with the parent who is present. Likewise, their responsiveness may be delayed. Sometimes, they may also call out for the absent parent, not understanding why their mother or father isn't present or doesn't respond. You may also notice clinginess right before or after a transition from you to your ex-wife or vice-versa.

What to do: Stone says the best response is constant reassurance. Consider making statements like, "Mommy and I love you very much. Just like you spend time with mommy, now it's time to spend time with me." Explain to them in terms they can understand that they will soon see their mother. Walk them to their bedroom. Read them a story while they're in their own bed. If they become upset when you leave the room, sit on the floor and wait for them to fall asleep. Make sure they have a special security object like a favorite stuffed animal or blanket that they take back and forth between homes.

Children (two to five years-old)

How they feel: More than likely, children at this age have only known one home and experience security in familiar surroundings. Stone says frequent and even simple changes regarding where they sleep, their eating patterns and how they're cared for can make them feel insecure.

How they act: Those who have trouble adjusting can become more irritable than usual. A good example is becoming upset because they have to drink out of a different cup than when they're at their mom's house or don't have their favorite stuffed animal by their side when going to sleep. "Children who innately have less flexible temperaments will experience greater difficulty going through a divorce," says Stone.

What to do: Make sure children pack their security or favorite objects when spending time with you. Or have them pick out things like a cup, plate or stuffed animal that they will routinely use when staying with you. Since change can be scary for young children, try to stick to established routines like eating meals and going to bed at the same time or watching the same TV shows or favorite movies. It will help them feel more secure.

Children (five to nine years-old):

How they feel: They may feel torn between you and your ex-wife, wanting to please both but find it difficult to do so when you and your ex are in conflict with each other. When children are in a no-win situation, they are likely to act out.

How they act: "Understanding and verbal expression have expanded and there may be more questions, sometimes the same ones repeatedly asked," says Stone. Since they also attend school, they're also more prone to stress - from teachers, other caregivers, classmates or friends - and may even absorb some of your and your ex-wife's stress.

What to do: Emphasize that it's perfectly fine to have a relationship with you and their mother even though you and your ex may have trouble relating to each other. Encourage them to talk about how they feel – or draw pictures – about being caught in the middle. When children can verbalize thoughts and feelings, Stone says they're less likely to act them out.

Preteens (10 to 12 years-old):

How they feel: They start to show more interest in friends than family and feel more independent. Oftentimes, they will prefer to spend more time with their friends, even if it cuts into the time they spend with you. They'll start to abandon old habits like sitting on daddy's lap and may feel embarrassed by outward expressions of affection.

How they act: Expect conflicts to arise between your expectations of spending time with them and their desire to be with their friends. Stone adds that they may also be distracted in school and less responsible when it comes to completing homework.

What to do: Emphasize that even though it's hard for them to concentrate right now, they are still expected to do their best. Consider informing their teachers or principal about your divorce so they can be better prepared to deal with your child's potential behavioral changes. Also realize that they're growing up. Give them the space they need to make small mistakes, solve problems on their own and discover new interests.

Teenagers (12 to 17 years-old):

How they feel: Not surprisingly, these children are more concerned with how your divorce is going to affect them, how their lives will be changed. At a time when they're defining their own identity, a divorce can challenge this process. At the same time, they may experience more stress because they may need to assume more household chores, move to another school, get a job or even relocate to a new home. They are also acutely aware of any financial losses or strains.

How they act: Common behaviors include resisting or refusing to do what you ask, moodiness, arguing with you more, taking sides with the "right" or the "wronged" parent, refusing to see one parent, poor concentration on school work, which can lead to a drop in grades, or blaming one parent for the divorce. Sometimes, they may even refuse to come home or come home late in an effort to assert their independence. Stone says that children who have witnessed their parents lose control – emotionally or physically - may simply copy their role models or be fearful of emotional expression, unaware that it can be modulated and shared without triggering a strong emotional response from another person.

What to do: Don't let your children get caught in conflicts between you and your ex-wife or place them in situations to choose sides. Encourage them to talk with you about their emotions – why they may feel angry, depressed or sad. No matter what they say, they have a right to their feelings. Don't judge them, dismiss their feelings or make them feel there will be repercussions for being honest.

As a divorced dad, understand what your children are feeling and don't be surprised if they act out in the ways mentioned above. Just remember that you can play a key role in helping them get back on the right track.

"Children whose parents focus on the negative aspects of divorce are less likely to value commitment, believe in the possible longevity of marriage and instead, perceive relationships as a disposable commodity," Stone says. "Children can learn that even when things fall apart, new things can be created."

Transitions can be positive and full of opportunities. Moving to a new home or spending time with dad at his new home is a good example. If you're the one who's moving out, narrow down your search to two or three places. Then involve your children in the final selection process. Point out their bedroom. Get their opinion as to which home they prefer since they will be living in it, too, explains Ron May, Ph.D., a licensed psychologist and psychology instructor at the University of Wisconsin.

They may even get excited, depending upon your approach. You can say things like, "Since you'll be closer to school, you can sleep 10 more minutes in the morning," or "You'll be closer to your new friend's house," he says. Maybe there's even a boy or girl their age living next door or down the block.

"Look on the positive side," he says. "Kids will be focused on the losses. You don't want to minimize or deny them but there are gains in a transition in family life. To point out what the gains would be is helpful."

After moving in, you can also teach your kids new skills. Many children enjoy doing the same activities with their parents. Consider making pancakes together. Maybe adopt a dog and spend time training the animal. Or go for long drives. He says driving offers a great opportunity to talk with teenagers. Since you can't maintain direct eye contact with them while driving, he says the emotional indirectness is often appealing to them and avoids conversations from getting overly intense.

Regardless of how you spend your time together, it's still important to set limits and expect your children to behave appropriately. Sometimes, he says dads get confused about enforcing rules. They think that letting their child off the hook is a good way to build a strong relationship with them. Or, when they're at dad's house, they don't have any responsibilities and can do pretty much what they want. Not true. In fact, May says a lackadaisical attitude usually has the opposite effect. You need to be their father first, not their friend.

So when it comes time to discipline, push aside guilty feelings. If your divorce is still fresh, your children may have intense feelings, such as anger. Confrontations may occur. What you need to do, says May, is lower their level of arousal. Sending them to their room, for example, can give them time to calm down. Then start a discussion about why they're misbehaving, acting out or so angry.

Watching their moods can also give you some indication about whether you're being manipulated. Does your young daughter snuggle up to you, telling you that you're the best dad in the world right before she asks you for money to buy a new sweater? Does your teenage son agree to clean his room before asking you to buy him a new computer? Are they in bad moods when you ask them to do something or turn down their requests?

"Sometimes, if you're feeling guilty or inadequate [as a parent] when you know you're doing the right thing, that's a sign you're being manipulated," May says, explaining that you'll know you're being played when your children display out-of-proportion emotions that may include excessive charm, affection, anger or guilt trips.

As a parent, you're there to serve your children's needs, not your own. Your children are not there to take care of you so be very careful about parent-child boundaries. For instance, don't expect your child to be your therapist, housekeeper, cook, buddy or ally against your ex-wife. May recalls one father who just broke down in tears at dinner with his children. He thought it was appropriate to share his feelings with them, that he was being a good dad by doing so. However, May says it's actually improper because children aren't equipped to handle such situations and become very uncomfortable. Worse yet, it can also set up a pattern where your children feel it's their job to care of you.

The idea is to be psychologically and emotionally present in your child's life. Talk to their teachers, meet their friends, know what their interests are, understand what issues they may be facing and make sure you're always available to them.

"Be centered yourself and take care of our own kind of emotional business," says May. "Grieving the loss of your [marriage] without beating yourself up, having some balance and resolving it, will lead you to feeling more accepting of yourself and you'll have less of a need to compensate."

Going Solo

For years, judges in divorce cases typically granted residential custody of a couple's children to the wife. But that trend has been slowly changing. Roles are reversing. In some cases, fathers are given primary custody of their kids, which introduces a whole new set of challenges for men.

Rich

When Rich and his wife divorced after 22 years of marriage in 1992, they had three children. At the time, his daughter was nine years-old, his middle son was 13 and his oldest son, who was living overseas in the military, was 20. Both Rich and his ex-wife decided that he would be better equipped to raise their two youngest children.

So mom moved out of the couple's home, finding a new place less than five miles away. Rich, who held a full time job as a computer programmer, stayed in the home with their children.

He quickly discovered all of the obstacles facing single parents. Finding a babysitter after school that he could afford was very difficult. So was keeping the house clean, doing the laundry, finding time to grocery shop, paying bills, making dinner, helping his kids with their homework, mowing the lawn, shoveling the snow and taking care of the dozens of other details required in keeping house and raising a family.

Rich assigned chores, such as doing laundry, to each of his children, which he says became a real problem. They expected that their clothes would "magically" appear in their dresser drawers, clean and folded.

"I said, 'You guys got to pitch in,'" he recalls. "It was a real change for them. There was a huge learning curve."

Still, Rich's primary concern was socialization. He wanted his children to form healthy relationships, despite the fact that their mother barely saw them two years after their divorce. He was especially worried about his daughter. Living in a male dominated house over the years with an absentee mother, she didn't have a role model or another woman to ask for guidance. So he set out in search of a surrogate mom.

Both of his kids latched on to a neighbor, a friendly woman whose son was the same age as Rich's son. Then Rich persuaded his daughter to join the Girl Scouts so she could socialize with girls her own age, connect with their mothers, attend events and have fun at sleep-overs. He says all of these activities helped his daughter slowly climb out of her shell roughly five years after his divorce.

Meanwhile, Rich spent a lot of time with his kids. They all learned to swim at the community pool, played games at home, watched TV, read together, planned vacations and traveled to fun places. It was his way of showing them his unconditional love and support.

So was disciplining them and making them honor their commitments. Anytime his children wanted something special, they discussed and created a plan. His son, for example, wanted a skateboard. Since he was performing very poorly in school, Rich came up with a very clever idea. He drew a picture of a skateboard and divided it into more than 30 white squares, which represented the number of days left in the semester. Every time his son completed his homework on time, Rich colored in one of the squares. Each day he didn't, the square would then be converted back to white. He told his son that once three-quarters of the squares were colored, he would buy him a skateboard.

His son did pretty well for almost two weeks, then stopped doing his homework. Rich wouldn't budge. No skateboard. He even burned the skateboard drawing to emphasize to his son that he had not fulfilled his end of the deal. Seeing the paper in flames evidently motivated his son to get back on track. He started doing his homework on time and by the end of the semester, had met his obligation and got his skateboard.

Rich paid attention to all aspects of his son's and daughter's life. He knew their friends, helped them change unhealthy patterns of behavior when possible and made sure they stayed connected to his side of the family for family support.

"Let your children know that you're always lovingly concerned," says Rich, a M3 member who's 64 years-old and has a good relationship with his children who are now grown. "We always had the rule of, 'I've got to know where you are and have to be able to get in touch with you if I need to be'. There were consequences when this rule was broken."

Ground Rules

Establishing firm boundaries or rules is very necessary, particularly for children going through the divorce experience, adds Arthur Kovacs, Ph.D., a licensed psychologist in Santa Monica, Calif.

"They get wired with anxiety," he says. "There are a lot of uncertainties they have to deal with. Their future seems unclear to them. What the rules are of who's going to be where and when and who's in charge of what are terribly unclear. So structure, rituals, boundaries are even more important than for ordinary kids. It will calm them down."

Likewise, if their mother becomes a part-time parent, be very selfless, says Kovacs. Make statements like, "It's not that your mother doesn't love you. We made a decision together that I'm able to be more responsive and care for you right now. Your mother isn't really leaving you just because she moved out of the house."

Even if your ex-wife virtually abandons your children, still frame it in a positive way. Search for words that make her look good as a mother. You can say things such as, "She decided you really needed somebody who would be there for you, in your corner, be able to love you and be consistent. She recognized that she was having trouble doing that. She's going to work on it and get better as time goes on but for now, she wants you to stay with me, where you will be always safe and loved."

Then reassure your children that you will never leave them. They may feel very insecure or afraid of being completely abandoned.

There will be many times where you'll be tempted – especially if your ex is outrageous or has abandoned your kids - to badmouth her to your children. You may try to explain that she's the problem, she's the reason your family has split up. You desperately want your children to know that you're the good guy and insist on their loyalty. But don't do it for the sake of your children. "Bite your tongue until it becomes bloody," he says.

Even in-laws can sometimes spell trouble. If they ask to see your children, assess the situation. Do they support your wife and hate you? Or are they in your camp? Look at their underlying motive. If they genuinely love your children and want to help out, then yes, allow them to do so. But if there was a nasty custody battle, watch out. They could try pumping your children for information that could be later used against you in court. Worse yet, they could also badmouth you to your children behind your back. Before you know it, you're back in court, facing yet another round of custody issues with your ex.

Being a great dad is a huge responsibility so you need to get over your pride and ask for practical help. Maybe a friend or neighbor can babysit once in a while or a relative can run errands. You can't do it all. Super dads are the stuff of fiction.

"It's an enormous challenge," Kovacs says. " Caretaker burnout is your biggest risk. Self-care is very important. Find anything that will give you some relief."

Did you know?

- There were 1.8 million single custodial fathers in 2008
- 51 percent of single custodial fathers are divorced
- 16 percent of single parents who live with their children are men
- 8 percent of single custodial dads raise three or more children younger than 18
- 36 percent of custodial fathers have child-support agreements or awards
- 43 percent of custodial fathers received all child support that was due
- 66 percent of fathers praised their children younger than six three or more times a day, according to a 2006 study

Breaking the News

Telling your children that you and their mother are divorcing can be a fairly traumatic experience for them. Ron May, a psychologist in Madison, Wis., offers several tips that can help minimize their pain, anger and fears.

1. It takes two: Ideally, this should be a joint effort. Both you and your wife need to sit down with your children and explain your divorce from a "We" perspective. Example: "We tried to make our marriage work" or "We have not been able to solve our problems so we are choosing to get a divorce".

2. Show respect: Don't blame each other for the divorce, start arguing or pit your children against your future ex. That approach doesn't help anyone and may only serve to escalate your children's negative emotions.

3. Emphasize your role: Tell your children that they're not losing their father. You'll still be involved in their lives and spending time together. If you're going to be moving out of the house, remind them they can call you anytime. May says kids are concerned if their dad will be emotionally available, whether you'll be there when they need you.

4. Give them space: After you break the news, don't be surprised if your children run out of the room and into their bedroom, slamming the door behind them. Wait at least 10 minutes before knocking on their bedroom door. Allow them enough time to process the bad news before you attempt to calm them down.

5. Constant Reminder: If you're moving out of the house, sometimes it helps to give children a special object of yours like an old watch, necklace or touchstone. It may help them feel your presence and stay better connected to you.

Children's Bill of Rights

We the *children* of the divorcing parents, in order to form a more perfect union, establish justice, insure domestic tranquility, provide for the common defense, promote the general welfare, and secure the blessings of liberty to ourselves and our posterity, do ordain and establish this Bill of Rights for all children.

1. The right not to be asked to "choose sides" or be put in a situation where I would have to take sides between my parents.
2. The right to be treated as a person and not as a pawn, possession or a negotiating chip.
3. The right to freely and privately communicate with both parents.
4. The right not to be asked questions by one parent about the other.
5. The right not to be a messenger.
6. The right to express my feelings.
7. The right to adequate visitation with the non-custodial parent which will best serve my needs and wishes.
8. The right to love and have a relationship with both parents without being made to feel guilty.
9. The right not to hear either parent say anything bad about the other.
10. The right to the same educational opportunities and economic support that I would have had if my parents did not divorce.
11. The right to have what is in my best interest protected at all times.
12. The right to maintain my status as a child and not to take on adult responsibilities for the sake of the parent's well being.
13. The right to request my parents seek appropriate emotional and social support when needed.
14. The right to expect consistent parenting at a time when little in my life seems constant or secure.
15. The right to expect healthy relationship modeling, despite the recent events.
16. The right to expect the utmost support when taking the time and steps needed to secure a healthy adjustment to the current situation.

Source: JT Spaulding Associates, LLC, Cary, NC www.divorcehq.com

Resources:

Top 9 Books for Helping Kids Through Divorce
About.com - Fatherhood
http://fatherhood.about.com/od/divorceddads/tp/divorcecope.htm

Top Ten Tips To Help Your Child Through Divorce
www.divorcewizards.com/Top-Ten-Tips-To-Help-Your-Child-Through-Divorce.html

Ohio State University Extension
Factsheet: Divorced Dads – Making the Most of Visitation
http://ohioline.osu.edu/hyg-fact/5000/5309.html

Parents Without Partners
www.parentswithoutpartners.org
Organization provides single parents and their children support, friendship and parenting techniques.

Parents Without Partners
 Practical Parenting…Tips To Grow On
www.parentswithoutpartners.org/Support2.htm

Divorced Father's Network
www.divorcedfathers.com/DFN/index.php
While the network targets fathers in California, it also offers an online learning center and member forum along with a radio show streamed live on the Internet

Divorced Dads
www.geocities.com/Heartland/Meadows/1259
Discussion forum

divorcehelpforparents.com
www.divorcehelpforparents.com
Website offers a monthly newsletter and tips on being a long distance dad, fair fighting, dating and more.

GreatDad.com
www.greatdad.com/category/397/divorced-dads.html

A parenting resource from the father's point of view. Website offers parenting advice along with a dad's blog and father's forum.

Daddy Brain
http://daddybrain.wordpress.com/2009/03/27/resources-for-divorced-dads/
A website devoted to divorced dads, offering resources, daddy blogs, education, a radio program and more.

Ex-Etiquette for Parents
Good Behavior After a Divorce or Separation
http://books.google.com/books?id=TcYsdsuEUiUC&pg=PA15&lpg=PA15&dq=letting+go+of+anger+divorce&source=bl&ots=vJAzOY-lPD&sig=u_5LELvl9V0NjS_UodUvNjhlRpI&hl=en&ei=XcEZSpWUNoP8swOM1ITgCA&sa=X&oi=book_result&ct=result&resnum=8#PPP3,M1
(Most of this 304-page book can be downloaded for free)

CHAPTER 5 -

Back to Being Single

I T'S A SATURDAY night around eight o'clock. You've got nothing to do. Nowhere to go. No one to call. You're tired of sitting in front of your TV watching crime shows.

You've been divorced for a few weeks, maybe even several months, and don't know how to get out of this rut. You wake up. Go to work. Come home. Eat dinner. Watch TV. Go to sleep. Then it starts all over again the next day. Other than your co-workers, you really don't socialize with anyone. How do you meet people? Where do you go to have fun? How do you start enjoying life again?

Living life as a single man again will take some adjusting. Don't beat yourself up if you suddenly find yourself without a social network. It's not uncommon for men who've been married for years to suddenly discover they have few, if any, close friends. Between working and taking care of their family, you probably didn't have much time for anything else.

But things are different now. Your kids may be grown or are teenagers, doing things on their own, or younger and living with your ex-wife. Either way, you have more free time than ever imagined. But you spend most of it alone. Weekends are the worst. Your feelings of loneliness and depression can be difficult to handle at times, perhaps overwhelming.

Just like other divorced men, you can do more than survive. You can start enjoying life once more. It may be hard to believe right now but it can happen. It's all up to you. What are you doing to change things? Are your establishing new routines? Are you reaching out to make new friends? Or, are you sitting around feeling sorry for yourself? Are you waiting for people to come to your rescue? Are you drinking excessively to numb painful feelings?

There are plenty of options as to how you can move forward, better face the days ahead and be happy again. But you must make the first move.

You're your own remote control. You have to get off the couch, out of bed, off of that old, ratty chair and take action. No more self-pity, pouting or sulking. It's time to get on with your life.

Start Your Engine

It's perfectly normal to feel angry, depressed or other strong emotions following a divorce. Since women tend to initiate divorces, this may have been something that was forced upon you. Perhaps you didn't see it coming or looked the other way. Divorce can be demoralizing and debilitating, making you feel as if you've been short-changed.

While divorce is often a tragic event, there's nothing more tragic than avoiding the opportunity to learn from this difficult experience, says Michele Weiner-Davis, a licensed clinical social worker in Boulder, Colo., who's also author of, Divorce Busting: A Step-by-Step Approach to Making Your Marriage Loving Again.

Now is the time to take a personal inventory, she says. No matter how mad you may be at your ex-wife, consider what role you played in the demise of your marriage. This isn't about blame. It's about understanding how you may have contributed to the downfall of your marriage. So ask yourself, what did your ex complain about? What did she accuse you of or argue with you about? Could there be a grain of truth in what she said?

"It's really hard to see the forest for the trees when someone calls you controlling and you don't feel you are controlling," she says. " I've counseled men whose lives have been disrupted by their wives filing for divorce. For the first time in their lives, they're willing to do some soul searching and recognize that in fact, they were making independent decisions and not willing to collaborate. They weren't listening to their wife's feelings about how to spend free time, budget issues or how to raise the kids. Ultimately, everything needed to be done their way. So a lot of these guys became more open, gentle and collaborative as a result of having the bottom drop out."

What's so devastating for some men is that they're totally in the dark about how they got into this situation. So they consider seeing a therapist or read self-help books for answers.

But another good resource are marriage education seminars, which teach you how to understand the dynamics of relationships and place yourself in the other person's shoes - whether it's your child, ex-wife or future wife - so you can find solutions to difficult situations. Weiner-Davis says many of these seminars are useful for individuals, not just couples in a rocky marriage. So don't exclude yourself because you're divorced. She says a lot of men start feeling better because they develop invaluable skills and learn how to do the dance a little bit more effectively whether they're in a relationship or not. [Check out www.smartmarriages.com for a listing of nationwide seminars.]

In the meantime, here's a technique that will help you kick-start your new life. Weiner-Davis routinely poses this scenario to many of her clients: Pretend you went to sleep tonight and a miracle happened. All of a sudden, your grief or pain is behind you. When you wake up the next morning, you feel much better and can move on with your life. What would you be doing that would be a sign that this miracle happened?

She asks people to envision their future life without the problems they're currently experiencing. In other words, when you're happy, what kinds of things would you normally do on the weekends or weekday evenings? She asks them to develop a list that could include activities like learning to play golf, taking a cooking or art class, joining a softball team or spending time with old friends.

"The first step in making this change is being able to envision it happening, then identifying the really concrete steps along the way that will be landmarks that progress is being made," she explains.

But watch for embers rather than fireworks, she says. Pulling yourself out of this rut is going to be difficult. So celebrate the small victories. Give yourself kudos for any small step you take that leads you to a better place.

Likewise, don't allow your mood to dictate what you do. More than likely, you're going to feel lousy for a while. Expect it. "Don't allow feeling down to slow you down," Weiner-Davis says. "Force yourself to do things. Research shows that the quickest, most efficient way to change how you feel is to take action, not sit around contemplating your navel or analyzing your divorce to death."

Just one word of caution: it will take some time to feel happy again. Still, don't wait to do things until you feel better. That could delay your emotional progress. She says there's nothing wrong with feeling bad at times since it can result in a growth experience. You may learn to like or even respect yourself more, enjoy living alone or for the first time in your life, feel whole.

Bill

After being married for 30 years, Bill, a retired high school teacher and M3 member, divorced his wife in 1998.

Living alone was challenging at first. When he came home, there was no one to talk to, confide in or just sit around with and watch TV. But on the upside, there was also no more arguing, no more feeling awkward or uncomfortable in his own home. So for Bill, his divorce actually created a more peaceful existence.

"My wife and I lived in the same house but we didn't share a life together," says Bill. "I'm of the generation that once you got married, you stay married. In the process of getting help, I was told I could only be half the problem. When I approached my wife on that, she did not take any responsibility of there being problems in our marriage. That's when I knew it was really time to get out."

When married, he says he had many acquaintances but no real friends. After his divorce, his social network expanded 1,000-fold. He also volunteers as a handyman for shut-ins and the elderly, has dated the same woman on and off for years, now enjoys a better relationship with his grown children and actually prefers to live by himself.

"I have a great life," Bill says. "I've got more friends than I ever had in my life. My divorce allowed me to become myself. Whatever happens to you, there is a positive side. That's what you should look for and work toward making yourself happy."

Mind-Body Connection

When counseling men who've recently been divorced, Michael Carolla focuses on three areas: physical, mental and spiritual development.

As a licensed marriage and family therapist and executive director at Touchstone Counseling Services in Pleasant Hill, Calif., he says many men are stressed out and often lose track of taking care of themselves. Some haven't cooked in years so they become fast-food junkies. Others stop exercising or don't get enough sleep. A handful finds solace in alcohol or pills.

Among your first step in adjusting to your new single lifestyle is to take care of your body, which is something everyone knows is important to do but doesn't always practice.

Do at least 30 minutes of cardio exercise several days each week. You probably won't feel like exercising so force yourself to do it unless your physician says otherwise. Consider jogging, swimming, bike riding or walking at a fast pace. But don't confuse cardio exercises with weight lifting. Cardio exercises elevate your heart rate, which in turn, reduce stress, help you sleep better, give you more energy and offer temporary relief from depression and anxiety.

Here's why: stress depletes the production of serotonin, a brain chemical that makes you feel good or enhances your sense of well-being, says Carolla, adding that stress can also lead to depression, which in turn, may cause body aches, soreness and tightness.

Ever hear of a jogger's "high"? When doing cardio exercises like running, hormonal substances called endorphins are released into your blood circulation. They act like morphine, giving you a mild sense of euphoria.

When stressed, he adds that your brain also receives less oxygen. That's why you may not be able to think clearly. He says many of the divorced men he counsels often report that their thinking is frequently "fuzzy".

Through proper diet and exercise, you can give your body and brain a fighting chance to overcome what may be one of the most difficult periods in your life. So treat your body like a sanctuary, not a garbage dump.

Then connect with something larger than yourself. Attend services at any house of worship. Sit in a park under a tree. Gaze at the moon or stars in the night sky. Do yoga. Engage in any form of spiritual practice that gets you out of our own head for a while, forcing you to realize that everything in life is bigger than you, explains Carolla.

He recalls one man who began fishing after his divorce. He enjoys the serenity, feels connected to the water and fish and loses himself in Mother Nature. That was his form of spiritual practice that helped him step beyond the pain in his own private world.

Other times, it can also help to evaluate your perspective. Carolla points to a local minister who asked his congregation a series of questions during his sermon one Sunday morning. "How many of you are rich?" he asked. No hands were raised. "How many of you got up this morning and had a choice of what to wear to church?" Everybody raised his and her hands. "How many of you actually had a choice of what to eat for breakfast?" Once again, hands were raised throughout the entire congregation. "How many of you had a choice of cars to drive to work?" Same response. Then the minister said, "Ninety-five percent of the people in the world don't have these choices. Comparatively, you are rich."

Looking at the glass as half full can help you reorient your thinking. So can becoming a hero.

"In most instances, with the court system, visitation and other divorce stuff, attacks are going on," Carolla explains. "You take those slings and arrows, are beaten up, chewed up and spit out. If you turn that around, maintain yourself, take care of yourself, are present and healthy for your children, that's kind of a heroic thing to do. So you end up being a hero in this story for your kids."

If you're like most dads, your children are your top priority. You may not be able to see them as much as you want, have supervised visits, barely have enough money to support yourself, let alone your kids, or can no longer contribute to their college education. Your list of problems can be as many pages as your divorce record. "Life isn't fair," you often say. You're absolutely right. It's not. It may even suck. But you need to step up, man up, and be the hero so that your children get to know the best and healthiest you and receive all the intrinsic gifts you have to offer.

"They deserve it," says Carolla. "If you don't take care of yourself and you're not the best you can be with the best attitude and in the healthiest you there is, then your kids are going to get cheated."

Joe

Even the messages you repeatedly tell yourself can make a difference. Take Joe, who was divorced after 22 years of marriage. Each and every day following his divorce, he told himself that at some point in the future, things will get better, things will work out and he'll be a better person for it. He clung to that belief, latched on to the fact that life does change, which he says helped him get through each day.

He was often lonely, didn't really have any friends to speak of or people he could confide in and, since he felt ashamed of being divorced, he was too embarrassed to seek any type of therapy because in his mind, it would prove to the world that he was a failure. "I felt like I was in a place that I couldn't crawl out of," he recalls.

Still, he forced himself to move on so he could move past the most painful time in his life. As an example, he ran three to six miles every other day.

"I've always been an athlete," says Joe, now a retired high school teacher and M3 member. "I took care of myself physically that way. It was something I had done my whole life and something I was familiar with and could fall back on. Whatever frustration or pain I had, exercise seemed to help."

He also kept himself busy by developing new skills. Since he rarely turned on a stove, he forced himself to learn how to cook. He took private cooking lessons from the son of one of his colleagues, a 15 year-old culinary whiz kid. They went grocery shopping together where he learned how to pick out the freshest produce and meats, then learned how to prepare healthy and delicious meals. Joe believed that after spending all of those years exercising and taking care of his body, eating frozen meals that were usually high in sodium, chemicals and fat would have been almost sacrilegious.

Soon, he began creating his own recipes and cooking homemade meals. "I not only found that cooking was good for me physically, but when I cooked, emotionally, it took me out of my life. I got so involved in the kitchen that it became a comfort zone for me. It was brand new and I had to concentrate on it to put all of the ingredients together for something to come out in the end."

The youngest of his three children, who was living with him after the divorce, also became his priority. He cheered him on at all of his wrestling matches, packed his lunch every day and made homemade dinners.

Being proactive pulled Joe out of his slump. Several years after his divorce, he found the courage to undergo therapy where he learned how to normalize many of his issues and get the help he needed to grow as an individual. He says it took another four years before he finally stopped punishing himself and just as important, learned how to forgive himself. He no longer feels ashamed and realizes he is a good person, a good dad.

"Don't sit back, feel sorry for yourself or wait for something to happen," says Joe. "Go out there, face the world and do the kinds of things that help you feel good about yourself. Go out there and continue to live life."

Anger and Forgiveness

Everybody heals at a different pace. There's no magic time frame for when you should stop being angry, feeling guilty or blaming yourself. So don't compare yourself to a coworker who only needed several months to regroup after his divorce or a neighbor who was divorced last year and still cries himself to sleep. But if you get to the point where you feel life is just too hard, that you're not able to function in key areas of your life, then it's time to seek help.

In the meantime, there are common traps to avoid like excessive drinking. Although getting repeatedly drunk temporarily makes you feel good or even have fun, its destructive power, namely alcoholism, will just add to your existing problems, not fix them or help you heal. Other times, gambling can play a devastating role. Not being able to fulfill your financial obligations – especially when it comes to your children - could cause you to become even more depressed with every poker hand played.

Establish healthy boundaries and search for positive influences that can help you shed your anger, forgive yourself or your ex and create a fulfilling life. For instance, don't be ashamed to temporarily live with supportive family members during your transition, says Robert Marrs, a licensed marriage and family therapist who also manages Aurora Family Service, an outpatient clinic in Milwaukee, Wis.

He says parents, brothers or sisters can be incredible sources of support. However, some family members may unintentionally fuel your anger and resentment. Don't let them engage you in conversations that appear to be combative or attacking either your ex-wife or your past relationship with her. You would only be borrowing their anger or other negative emotions. Although what they say about your ex or former marriage may be true, it will only perpetuate the negativity that's currently in your life and drag you many steps backwards in terms of personal growth.

Instead, focus on new hobbies or activities and establish weekly routines. Call old buddies. Form new friendships. Volunteer. Any of these things can be therapeutic because you're now concentrating on other things beyond your pain or misery.

Marrs recalls one divorced man who bought a dog. "He said, 'This dog saved my life,'" says Marrs, explaining that the man now had someone to come home to and who consumes his time. Instead of feeling sorry for himself, self-medicating or frequenting bars after work, he plays Frisbee in the park with his dog and meets new people.

Men need best friends, says Marrs. But if it's not tied to an activity, he says men tend not to reach out to other guys. Still, it's important to do so even if you don't feel like it because it's part of the healing process. You now have people who care about you, who will listen to you vent your anger and frustrations so they're no longer bottled up inside.

"Make the choice of doing something with somebody," he says, adding that society doesn't really encourage men to socialize in this way. "Take a look at what your opportunities already are in your life. From there, say, 'What else do I need? What isn't in my life? What hasn't been in my life that I need again?'"

In the end, forgiveness and reconciliation with your ex-wife will become important issues. Sometimes, however, people forgive each other for the wrong reasons - they don't want to deal with conflict, says Christopher Habben, Ph.D., a licensed marriage and family therapist and also associate professor of marriage and family therapy at Friends University in Lenexa, Kan.

He refers to it as cheap forgiveness, a term borrowed from author Janis Abrams Spring, Ph.D., who introduced the phrase. Another example is men who recognize their serious mistakes but are nonchalant about them, never paying emotional restitution. They minimize their contribution to their divorce, allowing themselves off the hook much too easily.

Before people can honestly forgive themselves or their ex-wife, he says they need to have some clarity about the offenses they're forgiving.

Consider a man who cheated on his wife, which caused his divorce. The next step is to figure out what led him to the affair. Was it simply an opportunity for sexual pleasure or something that may have been modeled by his father or mother? Maybe he just wasn't happy in his marriage.

"Sometimes I see folks who make these decisions because it's easier for their ex-wife to get up and leave than it is for them to say they want out," he says. "They create situations where it's easier for her to leave because they're not strong enough to say things don't seem to be going well."

He says relationships are places where injuries happen. But if you invest in an injury, hold on to it for years with a firm grip, then you become its slave. To really forgive yourself means to make peace with the person you injured - your ex-wife.

That can take many different forms. You can send her a short letter or email saying something like, "I'm very sorry for the choices I've made that led us to this point. I understand your decision to get a divorce. I'm not trying to win you back but I wish it didn't happen. I recognize my part in hurting you and apologize."

If you're able to reveal to your ex what your contribution was to your failed marriage, and be sincere about it, he says that act will free you to move forward.

But if you believe you're the one who was wronged, he says ask yourself what is the hurt behind your anger. Since anger is a secondary emotion, Habben says it protects you from something that's painfully familiar or unresolved. Maybe it was your ex-wife who had an affair that led to your divorce and you're having difficulty forgiving her or getting rid of your anger. Think about it. Were your parents divorced? Did either parent abandon you? Maybe your own situation brings up uncomfortable childhood memories and feelings of being rejected or unloved.

Instead of being angry all the time, "Invite your demons to tea," Habben says, explaining that this is a Buddhist concept. "Realize you have a soft spot for rejection. Rather than constantly trying to keep at bay for fear of being rejected, invite the notion of rejection into your life more often."

That doesn't mean you ask to be rejected by those around you. When you feel rejected, instead of trying to hide it or allowing your anger to escalate, talk about it with friends or a therapist. The more you engage in this process, the more you encounter it, wrestle with it, face it head on, the more it will lose its power or control over you.

So dig a little deeper. Is the anger you feel toward your ex really about her or should it be aimed somewhere else? Oftentimes, he says men have unresolved issues with their family of origin. So they wind up replicating those same wounds with their wife who ends up paying the price of the hurt they experienced with their own family.

No one is perfect. You have a right to be angry with your ex-wife for anything she may have done to intentionally hurt you. But who's being hurt by your anger? Chances are, it's not your ex-wife. It's you. It doesn't matter what she did or didn't do, said or didn't say. By forgiving her, you're not agreeing with her actions or supporting her behavior. You're releasing destructive emotions that have been trapped inside of you that can cause poor physical or emotional health down the road. Think of it as your salvation, your right to be free of the past, of your ex-wife's behavior, of your relationship with her. There's no longer any need to hang on to that bitterness, hostility or despair.

You need to close this chapter of your life so you can move forward. Forgiveness is the way out. Forgiveness is the only route to helping you find peace and happiness, both now and in the future.

Warning Signs

1. Do you ruminate about your ex-wife or all the mistakes you made during your marriage? Is it interfering with your ability to function on a daily basis?
2. Do you frequently have difficulty falling asleep or staying asleep?
3. Do you experience frequent bouts of crying?
4. Have there been significant changes in your eating habits? Are you overeating? Have you lost your appetite?
5. Are you drinking or self-medicating more than usual?
6. Are you lethargic? Do you lack your usual energy?
7. Are you unusually irritable or angry, taking it out on the people around you?
8. Are you more withdrawn than usual? Have you stopped engaging in your favorite activities or spending time with family or friends?

9. Do you often entertain thoughts of suicide?
10. Do you make up excuses to contact your ex-wife or repeatedly drive by your former house, which is now hers?

If you've answered yes to any of the questions, please consider joining a support group or contacting a therapist to help you better cope with the emotional baggage you may still be carrying around from your divorce.

Source: Michele Weiner-Davis, licensed clinical social worker, Boulder, Colo.

Feel Better Foods

Consider including these foods in your diet to help relieve stress or improve your attitude and disposition:

- **Whole grain breads, pasta and cereal** are called comfort foods because they're mentally soothing. They make the brain produce serotonin, a brain chemical that makes you relax or feel good.
- **Spinach, kale, Swiss chard and other dark green leafy vegetables** contain B-complex vitamins, which prevent stress because they help make serotonin.
- **Almonds, pistachios and walnuts** pack a big punch. Almonds are loaded with vitamin E, an antioxidant that boosts the immune system, and also B vitamins, which help your body better tolerate stress. Likewise, pistachios and walnuts have been found to lower blood pressure, keeping your head and heart calm.
- **Asparagus and broccoli** contain folic acid, which helps prevent irritability, stress, fatigue, anxiety and depression.
- **Chicken and turkey** contain tryptophan, an amino acid, which can help you sleep better and elevate your mood.
- **Berries** are rich in antioxidants, which help stabilize levels of the stress hormone cortisol.
- **Cantaloupe and oranges** are rich in vitamin C. Long periods of stress can deplete vitamin C in your body.
- **Salmon** is rich in omega 3 fatty acids, which fight against stress hormones.
- **Turkey and tuna** are rich in tyrosine, an amino acid that boosts the levels of two chemicals in your brain – dopamine and

norepinephrine. They can help you clear your mind, become more alert and concentrate better.

- **Milk** contains antioxidants that help destroy free radicals (unstable molecules in your body that can cause disease and aging) related to stress.

---

12 Ways To Let Go of Anger

1. Give yourself permission to be angry. If you fight it, it will either get bigger or make you depressed or sick. Anger is a protective emotion, a natural reaction to a threatening situation.
2. Tell yourself that you have reasons for your anger, but you want to be smart in how you deal with it. Anger is our way of restoring our sense of power and control. You don't want to add to your problems with bad anger reactions.
3. Write down all of the reasons you're angry. Write until you can't think of another thing to say. This will help you sort out your thoughts and feelings. Do this every day, or at least 4-5 times a week, while you're going through your divorce and other stressful processes.
4. Get some exercise. Anger generates a lot of physical energy, and if you're not using your energy in an exercise program, it will make your anger harder to manage. This is absolutely essential.
5. List your fears, which may be driving your anger and making things worse for you. You might learn some things about yourself.
6. Picture a cartoon figure, monster or animal that matches how you feel when you're angry. Tell it thanks for trying to help (that's why it's there), but that it can't be in charge. This is called, "See It, Don't Be It." Picture the angry part of you chilling on a beach with a cool beverage.
7. Avoid a lot of negative talk about your ex-wife to others. This will feed your anger, and won't solve anything.
8. Remember why you married your ex-wife in the first place. Consider that you might not have been wrong about the good things in her.
9. Practice empathy. Put yourself in her shoes and try to see the situation from her viewpoint. You don't have to agree with her or condone her actions—just try to empathize.
10. Come up with a list of positive things you can do to make your

situation better, then channel the healthy protective energy of your anger toward completing those tasks.

11. If there are children involved, protect them from your anger. Avoid saying anything negative about their mom or sending messages to your ex through them. Believe in them and trust them to handle their parents' divorce in the way that's right for them. If any of your children are having trouble coping, seek counseling.

12. When you're feeling calmer from the above steps, write about what's good, right and working in your life. Focus on gratitude for good things in your past, appreciation for what is present, and optimism about good things that are to come. Do this kind of journaling on a regular basis. It will help with absolutely everything.

Source: Adapted from the book, "Anger: Deal with It, Heal With It, Stop It From Killing You," by William G. DeFoore, Ph.D., Institute for Personal and Professional Development, Addison, TX http://AngerManagementResource.com

More tips:

- Don't let your ego stand in the way of forgiveness
- Separate your ex-wife from her behavior
- Develop a mantra or phrase that you can use to calm down
- Start a grateful journal to help you put things into perspective
- Invite someone you recently met to lunch or dinner
- Forgiveness has four stages: hurting, hating, healing and coming together
- Understand that you're going through a grieving process
- The zinc and iron in beef can act as mood-stabilizers
- Avocados can lower blood pressure and help reduce anxiety
- Spinach and other foods with magnesium can help lower our stress

Resources:

About.com - Divorce Support
Divorce: Tips For Dealing With the Anger
http://divorcesupport.about.com/od/angerandconflict/qt/divorceanger.
htm

Ezine Articles
Life After Divorce – What Exactly Do People Mean When They Tell Me To
"Move On" After My Divorce?
http://ezinearticles.com/?Life-After-Divorce---What-Exactly-Do-People-
Mean-When-They-Tell-Me-to-Move-On-After-My-Divorce?&id=1117238

TroubledWith.com
Forgiveness: What It Is and What It Isn't
http://www.troubledwith.com/Relationships/A000000720.
cfm?topic=relationships%3A%20divorce

ehow.com
How to Forgive After a Divorce
http://www.ehow.com/PrintArticle.html?id=4455025

essortment.com
Learn to Forgive
http://www.essortment.com/articles/forgive-relationships_7501.htm

divorce.net
http://www1.divorcenet.com/bbs/ubbthreads.php?ubb=showflat&Numb
er=185807&page=2
Offers 75 different chat forums, including, "How to forgive a cheating ex-
wife"

Life123.com
Cardio Exercise
http://www.life123.com/health/fitness/cardio-exercise/index.shtml
Offers a collection of expert content covering cardio exercise and other
life topics

SelfhelpMagazine.com
http://www.selfhelpmagazine.com/index.php

An online support community that offers discussion forums, articles, podcasts and more on a wide variety of topics

American Dietetic Association
www.eatright.org
Offers nutrition information for consumers

Anger Management Resource
http://www.angermanagementresource.com/healing-anger.html
Offers a free, healing anger newsletter

CHAPTER 6 ~
Dating

I T'S DEFINITELY INTIMIDATING. At times, it can be down right frightening. Just thinking about it can cause many personal fears or doubts to surface like, "I'm not good- looking enough," "I'm not smart or rich enough," or "I'm not funny enough".

Re-entering the dating scene after a long absence is nothing like getting back on a bicycle. Expect to fall once or twice and accumulate cuts, scrapes and bruises along the way. You may even find it somewhat difficult to pick yourself up and continue peddling.

More than likely, many things have changed since you took a woman out to dinner or to the movies. The world is dramatically different now than it was in the past. Even your own life has experienced major adjustments and changes. What you wanted back then is no longer the same as what you need or desire now.

Although your divorce may have left a bitter taste in your mouth when it comes to relationships, the time will probably come when you want female companionship. You may not be looking for a new wife just yet, but may want to find someone special you can enjoy intimate moments with, confide in or simply talk with over dinner.

Before you pick up that phone or post your photo and profile on an online dating service, the first question you need to ask yourself is, 'Am I ready?'

You're not ready to start dating if:

- You're still grieving over the loss of your ex-wife or marriage. You must go through this process in order to move on.
- You routinely think about your ex-wife or talk about her to your friends, family and coworkers.

- You haven't forgiven your ex-wife or yourself. You may still be angry with her, even resent her, or hate yourself.
- You communicate regularly with your ex-wife. Are you calling more often than you need to? Are you making up reasons to hear her voice?
- You're in the midst of a nasty divorce, fighting over every thing big or small, including custody of your children or visitation rights.
- You're excessively drinking or taking drugs to mask or relieve your emotions related to your divorce.

There may be other warning signs but you get the idea. If you're still living in the past or not yet ready to let go, you're not ready to start a new relationship. You'll simply carry your emotional baggage from your former marriage to your new relationship and in the end, possibly sabotage that relationship or repeat the same painful experience.

Every man experiences the divorce process differently and at different speeds, so make sure you're done grieving, know who you are, feel comfortable with yourself and know what you want before getting romantically involved. Otherwise, it won't be healthy for you or fair for the women you are dating.

Fear, Sex and Compatibility

Following their divorce, men sometimes feel as if their wife abandoned them. If that's your situation, take an inventory of what you lost, says Bill G. DeFoore, Ph.D., a psychologist in private practice who founded the Institute for Personal and Professional Development in Addison, Texas. You didn't just lose your wife, but possibly your dream that your family would stay intact for the rest of our life, he explains. So if you're fearful of getting burned once more, start small. Find safe ways of being around other women without the intensity or pressure of dating. While it's natural to feel a bit anxious, he says if your anxiety is overwhelming, that's a sign you may need to slow things down or possibly back off dating for a while.

But if you are ready to date, DeFoore suggests considering this technique that others use for stage fright or public speaking anxiety: picture yourself feeling good and having a good time on a date. Make up your mind ahead of time that you don't have any expectations. Envision yourself relaxing and smiling, which is actually a type of mental rehearsal that helps reduce anxiety. Repeatedly tell yourself that you're going to have fun no matter what happens.

Now that you're thinking positively, use that same energy on your date this weekend. Unfortunately, many men initially fall into one of two categories: they either incessantly talk or never say a word. Either approach could have you home by eight o'clock that evening.

"I would encourage you to ask questions, reflect and try not to move the subject back to yourself," DeFoore says, adding that safe topics include work, hobbies or special interests. "Keep the focus on the woman you're with in order for you to get to know her and [show] that you're interested in her. A lot of times men are really interested but their social anxiety will cause them not to talk and the other person doesn't feel the man is interested when in fact he is."

But one subject that is taboo is your divorce. No woman wants to hear a man go on and on about his horrible ex-wife or how his children now hate him or disrespect him because of his ex. Also steer clear of local or world disasters. You're not CNN. Keep the conversation positive or upbeat, says DeFoore, adding that if your date wants to hear about crime, suicide bombings or corrupt politicians, she can always watch the evening news.

First dates also need to be short. Limit your time to a cup of coffee or brief lunch. Take several deep breaths. Tell yourself that the outcome of the date doesn't really matter. You're simply going to find out some things about each other. Nothing more. If you have greater expectations, you'll possibly set yourself up to fail or be disappointed.

Just remember, says DeFoore, that it's impossible for any individual to fulfill all of your needs. View dating as simply one component of your life. Other people around you like friends, coworkers and family members will also play important roles. Strive to achieve balance and develop realistic expectations about the women you date.

For example, if you prefer dating much younger women, realize that your story may not have a happy ending. If you're in your 50s and dating a 20 something year-old woman, make sure the relationship is based on common interests and mutual respect, not just physical attraction.

"Be weary that there are gold diggers out there who are very skilled at putting on a show," he says. "You don't want to get paranoid but be aware that it happens. It's a very real thing. Because of their sexual desire and loneliness, some men give away the farm."

Back in the late 1990s, one of DeFoore's patients was coming out of a 25-year marriage. It didn't take long before he began dating a woman 15 years his junior. His attraction to her was purely physical. She was very flirtatious, which he enjoyed when they met, and was far from frugal. Still, he ended up marrying her. But 10 years later after saying, "I do", DeFoore says they do nothing but argue. The husband no longer tolerates her flirtations with other men and has problems with her poor budgeting skills.

What did he expect? DeFoore says that when dating, people put their best foot forward. So any problems you see at the beginning of your relationship will usually grow or be magnified over time. So really examine key areas of compatibility. Are you religious but she's not? How do you deal with extended family? Is she close with her family while you're estranged from yours? Do you want more children but she doesn't? What's her attitude toward spending? Does it coincide with your own?

"Just one incompatibility can be a deal breaker," he says.

Once the relationship becomes sexual, everything may change. Expectations may accelerate. She may expect things to move ahead while you don't or she may enjoy a casual fling while you may want a more serious relationship.

"The ideal scenario is the relationship doesn't become sexual until there's a strong sense of connection, closeness and trust between two people," he says. "When you take off your clothes and have sexual intercourse with her, your heart is exposed. You emotions are there. It's a big deal and needs to be treated as a big deal."

Online Encounters

There are many places you can meet women where you won't feel pressured to impress anyone. But you must reach out or make the effort. No one will email or call. Get yourself out of the house and try something fun and new.

Consider volunteering for activities sponsored by the local church, synagogue or temple. Join a common interest group or club. Meet new people at the local gym. Go out with friends as a group to dinner, which can also be less intimidating. In any of these situations, your mutual interest will spark casual and comfortable conversation. You can just be yourself.

Nowadays, one of the most popular ways to meet women of all ages is through online dating websites. Consider dating and social networking sites like Match.com, Plentyoffish.com, Facebook, or Twitter, says James Houran, Ph.D., a Dallas-based psychologist and columnist for onlinedatingmagazine.com.

If you've never dated online, there are some things you need to know. Think of this as a crash course in 21st century dating.

While some websites are free and others charge between $30 and $50 a month, he says there are two kinds of websites: mega sites, like Yahoo. com, that attract millions of single people, and niche sites that cater to people with very specific criteria, such as:

- ChristianCafe.com
- DatemyPet.com
- SeniorFriendFinder.com
- DateaGolfer.com
- Hiphopsinglesconnection.com
- Sugardaddyz.com
- MustlovePets.com
- Militarysinglesconnection.com
- eHarmony.com

Houran adds that you can use any search engine like Google to type in your own criteria or interest, followed by the words "dating site" (example: techies dating site). More than likely, an online dating service catered to your specific needs will pop up.

If you opt to meet women online, Houran offers several suggestions:

- All dating sites require you to create a personal profile. When describing yourself and your interests, be honest and stay away from cliché activities like "Enjoy moonlight walks on the beach". Also solicit input from those around you, especially woman friends, to help define your personality. "You may do or say something that will date you, [make you] look really inept, kind of naïve and that's a turn-off," he says. "You want to come across polished, professional and convey a sense of economic and emotional security. That's what women are looking for."
- Many websites offer communication tools. Use those tools instead of your personal email address for safety and security reasons.
- Never reveal personal aspects about yourself within the first few weeks like your full name, address or place of employment because there are many online scams. Watch out for women who try to solicit information from you but rarely reveal anything about themselves. "Either the connection you think is there isn't or you're being setup somehow," he says. Likewise, he says never send anyone pictures of your children because many pedophiles prowl dating sites for such photos.

- Communicate with women online for at least one month before meeting them offline. When asking a woman out on a date, start slow. Take separate cars. Ask her to meet you at a coffee shop or restaurant for about 30 minutes. If there's chemistry between you, he says you can always extend the date.

- Relationships tend to move faster online that offline. Don't rush the process. Be careful not to read too much into a relationship or how it's developing. "In matters of the heart, always use your head," he says. "Never give in to your biological urges, at least in the beginning. It will always do you a disservice."

Houran says there are plenty of quality, single women you can meet online, no matter how fussy you are. However, just because you're a man, don't think you're not at risk. After a divorce, he says you may be in a vulnerable state of mind. You may overcompensate for the damage your divorce did to your self-esteem or ego by unnecessarily splurging on dates. Be aware that you can fall prey to your own urges or be easily setup by scam artists.

More tips: Don't let a woman's online photo determine whether or not you should meet her. As a licensed, certified, clinical social worker at Johns Hopkins Bayview Medical Center in Baltimore, Daniel Buccino points to two of his patients who followed this advice. One is now engaged to the man whose photo didn't attract her while the other married the person.

Try not to rely on emails or texting as your main form of communication. Instead, consider an age-old practice. Pick up the phone. He says too much online communication can leave you guessing as to how the woman really feels about you. You can't hear the tone of her voice or see important, nonverbal cues like her mannerisms or eye contact.

Electronic communication also makes it too easy for men to panic.

Why didn't she answer my email for two days? What does this sentence mean? Is she mad at something I said or did? "People get all freaked out," says Buccino.

He recalls one of his patients getting paranoid about a woman he met online. He didn't know how to interpret her email messages or understand why it took her several days to respond to his emails. His emotions grew so intense that his subsequent emails came on much too strong and extinguished a potential relationship.

"He went crazy about why she hadn't answered his emails or texts," he says, explaining that initially, the woman wanted to be his friend, get to know him better before developing anything serious. "But he got too caught up with trying to interpret the meanings and timings of her emails."

Buccino says some men overcompensate by also flooding women they just met with needy emails. Other times, they blame them for not quickly responding, then drop them. The lesson here is patience. There's no need to rush. If you demonstrate that you're needy, guess what? You'll attract needy women. If you prove to be irresponsible, you'll attract irresponsible women. As the old saying goes, you get back what you give and can end up in a relationship that quickly falls apart, says Buccino.

"Don't be desperate," he says. "Women are looking for more than looks and money. They're looking for reliable guys who are not creeps, not desperate, not stalkers and who aren't trying to fix them."

Marty

Marty, a M3 member who is 64 years-old, has been dating online for more than six years. He waited more than a year after his 33-year marriage ended before dating again.

His epiphany came after a coworker challenged his culinary skills, daring him to cook a roasted leg of lamb. He followed through one Sunday afternoon while drinking nearly two bottles of wine during the process. Then it hit him. "I just cooked this leg of lamb," he thought. "What the hell am I doing here alone by myself?"

Everyone at work suggested he use online dating services. He initially tried Yahoo.com but had trouble developing his profile. Describing himself was a bit difficult. So was figuring out his interests. He says he went to work, came home and slept. He had no idea what he liked or disliked anymore or what type of person he had become. After taking a self-inventory, he managed to put together a profile.

One of his concerns was meeting age-appropriate women. Within a week or so, his worries disappeared. He says he was both nervous and pleasantly surprised when a 50 something year-old woman responded to his profile.

Since then, he's had several online and offline relationships. One online relationship ended after several months because the woman lived over an hour away. Another lasted just 10 months because the woman appeared to have serious personal issues. He met another woman through a friend and dated her for three years. As it turned out, she didn't want to be in a committed relationship.

Marty learned a few things about online dating. He never asks women for their phone number since it may make them feel uncomfortable. He gives them his cell, not home, number. If he doesn't feel an immediate spark but the conversation is good, he still meets them at a restaurant or coffee house of their choosing. If he has a good time, he calls them again, asking them to go to a movie, which gives them more things to talk about on their date. The third time, he usually invites them to dinner. But if the attraction is not there on any level - physical, emotional or intellectual - he tells them the truth so as not to lead them on, and is always respectful, saying something like, "I'm glad we met, but I don't feel we're compatible."

"Everyone has his own criteria," Marty says, also a member of M3. "What I look for is if the lady says, 'Can we share the bill' or 'Can I leave a tip?' That tells me she's on the generous side and isn't afraid to share her wealth."

In addition to his online efforts, he tried something new roughly two years ago, which, admittedly, was a big step for him. He attended a Saturday night dance for people over the age of 40, sponsored by an organization called Stepping Out Singles. There was quite a crowd, at least 100 people, he recalls. Then his anxiety took over.

"I was standing there thinking, 'What the hell am I doing here?'" he says. "I felt so foolish. I was very reluctant to ask anyone to dance. I was standing around like a wallflower."

Just then a woman asked him to dance. Then another. Despite feeling uncomfortable, he returned the following week and the week after that. Now he attends almost all the dances to meet new women. Although he has dated a few of the women he met at these dances, so far nothing serious. But he always remains friends with them and continues to have fun.

Marty says that your former relationship with your ex-wife has nothing to do with the new women you will soon meet. That's an important point to remember. Every woman is different in her own way.

"They're still women," says Marty, now a retired technical manager. "We still don't understand them. But take the chance. You're under no obligation and can say, 'It's not working for me, I'm moving on.'"

Telling Your Kids

Since it's been a while since you dated, you really need to see how different personality types mesh with your own personality. Date multiple women instead of hooking up with the first woman who's nice to you or pays you a compliment. Don't be surprised if you discover that what was once a turn-on years ago is now a turn-off.

There's no need to tell your kids about any of your casual dates, especially if they don't live with you, says Lisa Thomas, a licensed marriage and family therapist in Denver.

But if you have residential custody of your children, always introduce your dates as friends. All you need to say is, 'Daddy is having dinner or going out with a friend'. Meet them at a different location other than your house, which is considered to be a safety zone for your children.

"If you start bringing someone into their safety zone, it's possibly going to raise some eyebrows," she says. "Based on their age, development and how long the divorce has been, you have to assess whether telling your children will be helpful or harmful."

With young children, explain your situation in terms they can understand. Consider saying things like, "It's very sad that the relationship between mommy and I ended. But it's not good for me to stay in the house all the time by myself. Going out with my friends and having things I can look forward to makes me happy. Remember how excited you were to go the zoo last week or to your friend's birthday party? I like feeling excited, too."

Still, try to avoid scheduling dates during the time your children are sleeping over (if they live with your ex) or even after they go to bed. Fewer problems are likely to erupt, such as the need to cancel a date if your child suddenly becomes sick.

Likewise, telling your children later about a relationship is better than sooner, Thomas says. However, if they're teenagers and suspect you're dating, answer their questions but don't give them more information than needed. "You don't want to give kids more than they can handle," she says. "You don't want to overload them.

Never talk about your sexual relationships or have overnights when your children are spending the night. Only introduce your children when the time is right--when your relationship has turned serious.

She suggests telling them you want them to meet someone who's become very special in your life. Explain that she's not replacing their mother - no one can – but is someone that makes you happy.

Even then, Thomas says keep the first meeting short. Plan an activity like lunch or dinner. Avoid touching your girlfriend or showing personal displays of affection. Don't put your arm around her at the dinner table or hold hands. Give your kids time to warm up to the idea that their dad is now romantically involved with someone other than their mother.

"Don't tell them how to feel about her or put pressure on them to feel guilty if they don't like her," Thomas says. "Warn your date that you may be somewhat distracted because you'll be running interference between your kids and her."

If your girlfriend also has children, avoid one big get-together for your first meeting. Introduce her to your children. The next time, meet her kids. Otherwise, Thomas says, your children and hers could be overwhelmed.

If your kids act out in front of your girlfriend or are rude to her, Thomas suggests following your normal parenting routine. It doesn't matter if you're at home with your kids or bring them along on a date, they need to learn what your expectations are and that their behavior has both rewards and consequences. So discipline them accordingly.

However, it's not your place to discipline your girlfriend's kids. You are not their primary disciplinarian or rule-maker, Thomas says. If they misbehave, sit there politely. If they say mean things to you, hold your tongue. Don't escalate the situation. Let your girlfriend discipline them. No matter how bad things get, don't leave because her children will get the idea that they control the situation.

"They may not love the idea that you're dating [their mother] and try to sabotage the whole thing," says Thomas, adding that it's not a bad idea to bring each child a small present, indicating that you want to be their friend. "This is like the parent trap. Let them know that their plan isn't going to work."

If your girlfriend starts spending the night, start slowly, when your children aren't with you. Then prepare your kids for the change in routine. Thomas says it's important to set up rules and boundaries. For example, if they suddenly barge into your bedroom while you're in bed together, enforce your new rules, such as knocking before entering.

No matter how hard you try to explain to your kids that you need a woman companion, sometimes they may feel left out, that this strange woman has taken their place in your heart. Make sure they understand that they will always be your No. 1 priority.

One way you can demonstrate this is to build a family calendar with your children, adds James Houran, a Dallas psychologist. Write all of your children's activities on the calendar as well as your own, such as your dates, when you may be going out of town or taking your mother to the doctor.

"Use one calendar for everything," he says. "It's amazing how much more it will put things into perspective for you. It allows you to spend time with people that otherwise, you aren't, and helps you constantly be in check. What do you need to pay more attention to? Where does your child need extra attention?"

Then develop a 48-hour rule, continues Thomas. If your teenage son forgets to put something on the calendar and calls you at the last minute for a ride to a friend's party, you can say you have plans, tell him to find another ride or offer to drop him off earlier or perhaps later to the party. This will help your children respect your time and better understand that you have other interests and responsibilities.

One last tip: Your children can respond well to your dating if your ex-wife supports it. Although seeking her approval may be an impossible task, Thomas still suggests asking. She may have started dating, too, and needs your support just as much as you need hers, especially if your children are upset about it. Ask her to say, "It's good that your daddy is trying to find someone who makes him happy." Offer to reciprocate. Even if she refuses, Thomas says, "It's always good to be the bigger person and do the right thing. Always take the high road."

Make It Last

There are thousands of women out there in every city across this country who may meet your criteria for a partner. But the most important qualifications are finding someone who loves you, whom you love and is able to be loved, who respects you, is kind to you and is willing to do the work when things get tough. If you can find a woman with those qualifications, then you'll discover the rest of the items on your wish list don't really matter, says Michelle Bohls, a licensed marriage and family therapist in Austin, Texas.

A lot of times, she says men who come out of a long term relationship or marriage get too close too soon.

"Oftentimes, men will get involved physically and bond with someone before they really take a look at who she is and if she's a good catch for them," she says. "The woman may be fun, make you feel good, but you won't look at the fact that she drinks too much, her work is her life or that she's really an unhappy person."

So pay attention. Don't form a relationship with a woman only because you're physically attracted to her, she needs fixing or wants to be rescued, which can make you feel important or powerful, she says. Face the facts. Don't gloss over major personality flaws or settle for second best.

Otherwise, you might find yourself moving from one bad relationship to another, one divorce to another.

Bob

If you're lucky enough to find true love a second or even third time, there are some things you can do to help ensure the relationship is long-lasting, says Bob, a M3 member who's 67 years-old.

Bob's first wife died from cancer after 18 years of marriage. His second wife divorced him after 14 years of marriage because she had difficulty coping with his long bout of depression following the loss of his job and unexpected passing of his father, brother, best friend and even dog within a several year period.

So he joined a divorce support group that was facilitated by a woman named Lois. Six months later, he says Lois developed a brain aneurysm and ended up at the local hospital.

"There was a spiritual push inside of me to see this woman," he says, adding that at the time, they were barely friends. "I spent time with her family through her surgery. Each day thereafter, I went to see her. That's how our relationship began."

Eight years later, the couple is still together. Although they live separately, Bob hopes their relationship will last as long as he does.

Here's partly why their relationship is so solid: He didn't start dating her until after he emotionally let go of his second marriage, which was more than a year following his divorce. He took his time getting to know Lois and didn't try to impress her, claiming to be someone he wasn't. He saw her at her very worst - after brain surgery covered with stitches - and still hung around. In time, he discovered that their personalities were compatible and that they shared similar interests. He listens to her, is loyal and doesn't try to control her. He makes her laugh, does nice things for her and always tells her the truth.

When he asked a woman friend out to dinner - she took care of his mother who had Alzheimer's - he told Lois about it so she wouldn't get the wrong idea. On three different occasions, he also surprised her with concert tickets for her favorite singer.

"Lois is like a wife to me," Bob says, adding that rushing into a relationship ranks among the worst things a man can do. *"I have no desire to meet any other women. We're very happy with the way things are now."*

Dating Tips

- Are you ready for your date? Take a shower, brush your teeth, comb your hair and wear clean clothes, not something picked up off the floor. Don't give her the impression that you're a slob or have personal hygiene issues.
- Are you on time? Don't be late. Don't be early. It's disrespectful. However, if something unavoidable comes up and you're going to be 10, maybe 20 minutes late, be courteous. Call her and explain. She'll appreciate it.
- Does your conversation resemble a monologue or dialogue? While sharing a few things about yourself, also take some time out and listen. Really listen. Find out what her interests are, which will give you good ideas for future dates. Make sure the conversation is two-sided.
- How many drinks did you order? No matter how nervous or anxious you may be, keep your drinking under control. Don't get drunk. Otherwise, she may get the idea that you have a drinking problem. Worse yet, she may argue with you about whether you're too intoxicated to drive yourself home and end up calling you a cab. Then you can call her, "long gone".
- How much money does she want? Never loan any woman you recently met money, no matter how real her sob story appears. New relationships are not business transactions. There are plenty of scam artists out there waiting to pounce on vulnerable men. If she asks for a loan and promises (cross-my-heart) to pay you back the next time you meet, make it a brief date, hang on to your wallet, then run.
- Are you focusing on her or the pretty blonde at the next table? Even if you're not attracted to your date, show some manners. Be polite and respectful. Make eye contact with her. Don't let your eyes wander around the room, staring at other women who may be sexier or better looking.
- Did you ask her for sex? Don't expect sex or be obsessed with

it on the first date. She may be turned off, thinking sex is your only agenda. If you push her on the subject, she may walk out. Who would blame her? Keep your zipper and mouth closed on this topic. Remember, your goal for the date is to get to know her and potentially start a relationship, not end it by her feeling disrespected.

- Did she ask for your phone number? Play it safe on a first date. Limit the amount of personal information you give anyone you just meet. If she asks for your phone number, don't share it if you have reservations. But if you decide to, don't lie. Consider giving her your cell phone, not home phone, instead. Likewise, no matter how much you like her, don't push her for personal information. Let it come naturally.

- What language are you speaking? Lose the four letter words and other potentially offensive language. It may be OK around your friends but not on a first date. Show some style. Show some class. Otherwise, you could ruin the evening with your potty mouth.

- Who's calling? If you're expecting an important call, let her know that your conversation may be interrupted. Otherwise, don't answer your cell phone. It's rude. That's why voice mail was invented.

- Are you both divorced? Talking about your divorce and ex-wife is normally taboo. But if you find that your date is also divorced, then it may be OK to share your experiences with each other. You may even find there's some shared humor in what you've both encountered.

Ideas for Inexpensive Dates

No money? No problem. Here's an article posted by David G. Mitchell (www.savingadvice.com/blog/2008/09/17/102634_101-inexpensive-dates.html) that offers 101 ideas for dates that don't require a savings withdrawal. Here's a sampling:

- Treat her to ice cream
- Go hiking or cycling
- Go to a driving range
- Attend a lecture, visit a museum
- Go to a church, synagogue or temple service together
- Take your dogs to a dog park
- Go food shopping, then make dinner together
- Go apple picking

- Go to a neighborhood garage sale or antiquing
- Go for a scenic drive or look at decorated houses at Christmas
- Accompany her when she volunteers for a charity event

Did you know?

- There are more than 800 online dating services in the US
- More than 20 million people a month visit online dating services
- With online dating services, the average ratio of emails to responses is 20 to 1
- Never talk politics or religion on a first date
- Did you have a good time on your date? Call her the next day to tell her.
- Spoken words only account for 30 -35% of a person's message. The rest is transmitted through nonverbal communication.

Resources:

About.com: Divorce Support
Opening Yourself up to Dating and Romance After Divorce
http://divorcesupport.about.com/od/romanceafterdivorce/Opening_Yourself_up_to_Dating_and_Romance_After_Divorce.htm

FamilyEducation
Dating After Divorce: What It Means For Kids
http://life.familyeducation.com/divorce/dating/29599.html

100 Best Dating Sites
Dating After Divorce: 50 Tips to get Back into the Groove
www.100bestdatingsites.com/blog/2008/dating-after-divorce-50-tips-to-get-back-into-the-groove/

Talk About Marriage
The Marriage and Relationship Forums
http://talkaboutmarriage.com/
Offers at least 20 forums, including the dating scene, general relationship discussion, dealing with grief and loss, going through divorce and separation and the men's clubhouse

TopDatingTips.com
How to Ask Someone Out: Get the Timing Right
http://www.topdatingtips.com/timing.htm

While there are many popular dating services, such as eHarmony.com or Match.com, here are several less known services you may be interested in:

Single Parents Mingle
www.singleparentsmingle.com
Devoted to parents without partners seeking friendship or romance.

Eight at Eight Dinner Club
www.eightateight.com
Matches four men with four women - based on their age, interests and background – who then meet for friendly conversation and dinner. Available to single professionals in New York, Chicago, Atlanta, Dallas, Denver and Washington, DC.

Date.com
SeniorFriend Finder
www.date.com
This website caters to men and women who are 50+. It's free and supports over two million singles.

FriendFinder
http://friendfinder.com
Designed for people who want friends but aren't quite ready for romance.

CHAPTER 7 ~
Remarriage

"I do."

T HERE ARE PROBABLY no other words in the English language that better symbolize love, commitment and perhaps a lifetime of happiness. But just the opposite can be true if these words are spoken to the wrong woman.

It's been at least a year since your divorce. Perhaps you've made new friends, developed new interests and dated a bit. You may have even found someone who has become very special in your life. You love her. She loves you. She seems to like your children. You like hers. You get along like Bourbon and water. So what's to stop you from proposing marriage?

Plenty. You know by now that it takes more than love and commitment to make a relationship work. Just look at your last marriage, which you thought would last forever. You've already been burned and don't want to go down that same painful path.

Second marriages can be much more complicated than first marriages for two main reasons: Kids and finances. So before you say those two magic words, think with your head for just a moment. Consider these questions:

Do you still have trauma or drama in your life related to your ex-wife? Are all aspects of your divorce settled? How about your children? Have visitation schedules been routine for a while or are you still going back and forth to court, suing for residential custody or child custody payments? What about your future wife's children? Will they be living with you? Do you know how to balance your time and energies between a new wife, work, your biological children and stepchildren? Ever ask about her credit rating? Is either one of you in serious debt, which could cause some friction down the road?

That's just the beginning. While your love for her may seem endless, so are the numbers of issues that can cause a happy marriage to sour. If you really love her, really want her by your side for the rest of your life, then do both her and yourself a favor. Spend some time talking about your expectations of each other. Be honest and open. You may even consider premarital counseling. The key is to make sure you don't repeat past mistakes or enter into a long-term, committed relationship for the wrong reasons.

Laying the Groundwork

It's important to figure out what went wrong with your last marriage so you don't make the same mistakes with your new wife. Just keep in mind that no couple is 100 percent compatible. There will be times where you'll disagree, even fight. You'll express differences in opinions. She may not like your friends. You may not like her cooking or taste in clothes. You'll never see eye-to-eye on everything.

That's why successful marriages are less about compatibility and more about how you manage your differences, says Greg Kuhlman, Ph.D., a licensed clinical psychologist and pre-marital educator in New York who also conducts a seminar called Marriage Success.

Differences don't have to lead to divorce. Although you probably learned many things from your last marriage, Kuhlman offers some of the teachings from his workshop that can help you set the stage for a healthy relationship.

For example, he points to research conducted by relationship guru John Gottman, Ph.D., co-founder of the Gottman Institute and director of the Relationship Research Institute. It shows that if any relationship is going to succeed, people need five times as much "positivity" as negativity from their spouse or partner.

That will also impact the way you interpret your partner's comments or action. Consider a couple that typically compliment each other. If the husband says, "Honey, I'm going to the store," her reaction will either be neutral or positive. She'll think, "He's doing me a favor. Now I don't have to go." But if there's too much negativity in the relationship, constant arguing, criticisms or put-downs, her perception changes. Now she thinks, "He's always trying to find excuses to leave. He never wants to stay home with me."

So if you want your marriage to remain happy, stay on the positive side. That means being intentionally positive, offering compliments or praise, even for small things. Likewise, limit the amount of criticisms.

While honesty in any relationship is essential, it doesn't always apply to small things like when your wife asks your opinion of her new blouse that you may not particularly like. Don't let every little thing in your head come out of your mouth, says Kuhlman.

But if you do have constructive criticism, use a "soft startup", he says, especially if there's a potential for your comments to turn into a "blamectomy". "Take the criticism and blame out of it as much as possible," he says. "It doesn't have to be particularly nice but you don't want to blow your partner out of the water."

Three more tips:

- Schedule sensitive communications at times when you're not already overloaded or exhausted like when coming home from work. Consider a Saturday morning or another time when you're more relaxed. But if you do get overloaded in the middle of a conversation, Kuhlman says use a time out, otherwise tensions may escalate. Tell your wife your blood pressure is rising and you just need to take a break for a few minutes. Walk around the block. Listen to music. Do anything that calms you down. Then continue the conversation or reschedule it later that day to avoid your wife thinking you want to avoid her or the topic.
- Plan one night a week as date night, which can help boost the positivity in your relationship. You don't have to spend a lot of money. Even walking to the nearby park or ice cream store counts. It also helps if you structure at least 20 minutes of time each day to bond with each other, he says. Turn off the TV. Talk. Listen. Spend quality time together, anything from bike riding to preparing dinner.
- Manage the negativity with your ex-wife. Uphold your part of agreements and try to develop a very structured arrangement so you're not always negotiating with her. Otherwise, it can cause tension between you and your new wife and kids, especially if they're caught in the middle.

"Learning about what makes marriage works is very helpful for a lot of people who've had bad experiences," Kuhlman says. "People who are divorced have a better basis for understanding this. There are good strategies you can use. You just have to learn about them, which [can be] very reassuring."

Double Trouble

One of the biggest problems for blended families is dealing with ex-wives who've been hurt, invade boundaries or try to exert some kind of control over their ex-husband or his new relationship, adds Lisa Brookes Kift, a licensed marriage and family therapist in San Rafael, Calif.

If your ex-wife is the vindictive type, she may also try to break up your new marriage. You can address the problem with her, but it may not do any good. So try to set guidelines like no unannounced drop-ins to your house or no excessive phone calling, she says. Don't participate in screaming matches or give in to temper tantrums, which could cause trouble between you and your new wife.

Never feed your ex-wife's drama, even if she is saying bad things about your new wife or does subtle things to undermine her. Empower your new wife not to respond, to place the needs of your relationship and children first. Do whatever you both can to take the high road and not let your ex rule your life.

Start the process by figuring out what you don't have control over, what you do, then put energy into the latter, adds says Christina McGhee, MSW, a divorce coach and parent educator in Houston.

"Sometimes, when second marriages occur, an ex may try to continue a negative cycle with intimacy," she explains. "If you don't passionately love each other, then she's going to put all of her energy into passionately hating you. So continuing the conflict is a way to stay connected with you. You've got to break that cycle by not responding."

Regardless of how bad things gets, one way to create harmony with your new wife is to include her in decisions regarding your ex-wife and children.

"A lot of times, what happens is that second wives are put into situations where their lives are really impacted by a lot of the decisions being made that they're included in," McGhee says. "Have that initial sit down conversation – you and your spouse - about how you're going to manage things. Have a united front."

Sometimes, your children may treat your new wife with disrespect, which can cause distress and upset your happy home. She says it's common for children to feel loyalty conflicts when dealing with stepparents, especially if they don't feel they received permission from their biological mother to accept her.

No matter how difficult the situation, don't put pressure on your children to love, like or even accept your new wife. McGhee says it's important to be patient, to give them time to build a quality relationship with her.

Many stepfamilies also plan everything together. Not a good idea. Children need alone time with each biological parent. She says your new wife will gain respect from your kids if she understands and supports their need to spend one-on-one time with dad.

Still, this scenario is very different than if your children try to distance themselves from you. If it ever gets to the point where your ex-wife tries to turn your children against you or your new wife, that's a whole different ballgame, McGhee says, calling it alienating behavior. She says it's important to get educated or professional support from a coach or therapist so you can understand the dynamics of alienation or hostile aggressive parenting, then learn how to deal with it so you don't make the problem worse.

For example, she says some parents get caught in the trap of fighting fire with fire. "If my ex-wife said this about me or my new wife, I'm going to set the record straight. I'm going to tell my kids my side of the story, tell them everything about what their mother did to me so they'll realize I'm the victim."

If you take this route, you're simply providing your ex-wife with more ammunition to use against you. Worse yet, your kids get stuck in the middle with no way out.

In essence, you're asking them to do something taboo - to choose between you and your ex-wife.

Give your children clear messages, says McGhee. Tell them they don't have to take sides. Explain that just because their parents are mad at each other doesn't mean they have to be upset with you or their mother. Let them know they have a right to feel any way they want, even if it's different from the way you or their mother feels.

Talk it over. Talk it out. Then be patient. Let the relationship between your children and your new wife develop naturally, over time.

"A lot of times, in the early stages of a second marriage, the drama takes center stage," says McGhee. "Don't let it drain the energy out of your relationship. Make sure you have a lot of communication in your current relationship."

But sometimes, the problem isn't your ex. It can be right under your nose without even realizing it. Your new wife may be jealous of your ex-wife for a number of reasons. At one point in your life, you loved your ex, may have had children with her and will always share a history together - not all of it was bad.

If you suspect this is what's happening, try to identify the behaviors or situations that are causing tension in the relationship. Maybe your current wife feels left out, that you spend too much time talking with your ex or that your children still haven't accepted her. Find out what's causing the jealousy. If your current wife is still struggling or feeling overwhelmed by jealousy, help her find support, says McGhee, pointing to websites such as www.secondwives.com or www.bonusfamilies.com.

Another consideration: are you sensitive about how much time you're spending with your children, new wife and step kids? While the key to relationships is love, love equates to attention, says Brett Williams, a licensed marriage and family therapist in Costa Mesa, Calif.

Since half of your love will be going in one direction – to your new wife – and the other half pulled in the opposite direction - toward your children - he says you'll be in conflict right out of the gate. Your new wife may unconsciously measure everything you do by the level of attention you devote to her and her children. Don't be surprised if she starts making comments like, "You love your children more than me."

"This is the trap you're in," Williams says. "The way to crawl out of it is to first understand the trap. Then make the conscious effort to make sure you're balancing your time. How many days each week are you spending with your kids, her kids?"

Consider keeping a mathematical record or journal because your new wife may do so. She may say, "You spent two days with your kids and 30 minutes with me or my kids." He says the debate about quality time versus quantity is "garbage". He says men tend to take their children's side and stop bringing attention to their spouse and her kids, which can create a split.

Instead, play fair. If you bring up a concern about your children, talk about a problem that your wife or her children may be experiencing. If you're teaching your son how to bat a ball, spend equal time with her son doing what he enjoys. Don't drag him to a park - with or without your son - to play catch or soccer if he hates sports. It won't be seen as love. Find out about his interests, his favorite activities.

Likewise, during holidays, be very clear with your new wife that you're going to give your kids your full attention. You may simply miss them or have limited opportunities to spend time with them. It's also OK to spend some alone time with your children, even on holidays. After Thanksgiving dinner, you may take them to the movies, for example. Just plan everything in advance so everyone knows what to expect. This way, Williams says your new wife will be much less inclined to feel slighted or shunned by you.

He says attention will govern everything in your relationship. So continue the same things you did when dating your current wife to avoid her feeling left out or ignored. If you went to the movies every Saturday night, continue the practice. If you gave her little love notes or cards, keep doing so, he says.

But you can go crazy trying to please everyone. While relationships don't develop overnight, there are some things you can do to move your new family along.

For example, make dinner a family activity. Get everyone involved in the process of preparing dinner and cleaning up the dishes. Young children can set the table. Rotate the position of cook and assistant cook. Everyone can also take turns clearing the table or cleaning the dishes.

Make sure to turn off the TV and cell phones. Go around the table having each person say something good or funny that happened to them that day. It helps them focus on the positive things going on in their life and places their attention on things that are going well instead of their gripes or adjustments they've had to make, says Williams.

Later on when relationships begin to build, consider placing one family member in the hot seat every now and then. Each family member has to say something nice about that person, what they like about them, perhaps something nice they did.

"The family has to interact on some project together to build that team or group mentality," says Williams, also author of, You Can Be Right Or You Can Be Married and creator of the Date Night Deck – 52 dates to connect, rekindle and deepen your love. "If they're doing everything fragmented – one kid is doing homework, another is watching TV, a third is outside playing – the family will stay fragmented. Giving them a task that they can all work on together will keep them building the mentality that you are a unit."

Vic

However, there may be times when kids become jealous of girlfriends or a new wife. Vic, a 58 year-old salesman in the transportation industry, says when he began dating the woman who is now his wife, his then seven year-old son viewed her as a threat. His son became jealous, perhaps even in competition with her, for Vic's attention.

"I was pretty open with him at the time," recalls Vic, also a member of M3. "I said nothing is going to change in our relationship. I'm not moving away. I reassured him that nothing would change between him and me even though this new person was coming into our lives. She would only add to our life, not subtract from it."

So when his son came for visits, Vic was certain to keep things fairly normal or routine as they had been in the past, despite the fact that his girlfriend wanted to impress his son with exciting activities. As time went on, Vic says he let the relationship between his girlfriend and son develop at its own pace. They got to know each other. They began liking each other and enjoying each other's company. His son's jealousy diminished with each visit. By the time Vic married her nearly two years later, he says they both got along fairly well.

Later on, Vic and his new wife had two children when Vic's son was about 13 years-old. Vic says he was immediately brought into their family. He held both newborns at the hospital, became a part of their lives the day they were born and enjoys being their big brother.

Now his son is grown and lives in another state. Throughout the years, his son's relationship with his stepfamily has remained close. In fact, every time he calls home, he typically spends more time talking to his stepmother than Vic.

Vic says fathers must be aware of the dynamics between their kids and their new stepfamily.

"Your child may feel threatened," he says. "Be aware of it. Don't ignore it. It won't go away."

House Rules

After being married, you may be living with your wife's children. Expect challenges. Transitions can be very difficult, especially if there aren't any rules.

"The guy often comes in and says, 'I'm here now. I'm going to be head of the household and you're going to listen to me,'" says Jeannette Lofas, Ph.D. and licensed social worker at the Step Family Foundation, Inc., in New York. "He moves too fast, too soon and the kids reject him. His new wife thinks he seems harsh."

So before you're married, create house rules for your stepchildren as well as your own children when they visit. Some examples could include:

In this house, we:

- Say, "Hello", "Goodbye", "Please" and "Thank you"
- Look each other in the eye when we talk to each other
- Treat each other with respect. We'll be teaching you what respect is and the different ways to show respect to people.
- Allow others to finish their sentences
- Make our own bed
- Leave the bathroom better than we found it – we hang up towels and don't leave toothpaste in the sink
- Clean our own dishes

While you or your wife can develop these rules, the key is that you must both agree to them and enforce them. Otherwise, there's no point. Your stepchildren will pick up on your disagreement and drive a wedge right between you and their mother, she says.

Also important: No decision trumps the other. You or your wife can't shoot from the hip, making up new rules or decisions as you go along. Lofas says to think of yourself as coaches who need uniform rules to guide your team.

More than likely, there will be many rules you will disagree about, says Lofas. So compromise and consider alternatives. For example, maybe your wife grew up in a family where she could keep her bedroom any way she wanted to because it was her own personal space. So your stepdaughter's room resembles a pigsty. But you can't stand the mess, seeing her clothes, shoes and other personal items laying all over the floor.

Don't bother fighting. Find a compromise. Come up with another rule that you can both live with like your stepdaughter must clean up her room once a week. The other six days won't matter. What's important is that the negotiation process doesn't negatively impact the relationship between you and your new wife.

Likewise, you must also agree on discipline or what punishment to administer if the house rules are broken.

"Discipline is the glue that holds families together," says Lofas. "Once kids know what is expected of them and that there will be consequences if they don't do it, then the family works much more smoothly."

Just make sure the punishment fits the crime. For example, if they don't make their bed, which is a house rule, then they must make their bed and two others the next day.

She says many parents love time out. But they send their children to their room that has a TV and a computer, which they turn on after closing their bedroom door. She offers a slightly different version of time out. Tell your children to sit on their bed for 15 minutes with the door open, the TV and computer off, which she says can be excruciating for any kid. Fifteen minutes later, they need to tell you what behavior they're going to change like they'll no longer swear at their stepfather.

As a stepfather, you may think your new wife is too lax about what behaviors she tolerates from her kids. Talk to her first before saying anything to your stepchildren. Tell her that you're uncomfortable with her kids calling her a bitch or with the disrespect they show both of you. Then develop a new house rule – if it doesn't already exist - such as, "We will not swear in this house," or "We will treat each other with respect at all times".

But what should you do if you try to punish your stepchildren and they say, "You're not my real father. You can't punish me. I don't have to listen to you."

Lofas offers a response: "You're absolutely right, I'm not your father but your mother and I have decided on these rules. So you need to go to your room, sit on your bed for 15 minutes and think about what you need to do differently." Then be firm. She says it may take a while for your stepchildren to get the message that you're in charge but once they see that their mother is backing your decision and you back hers, their acting out tends to diminish over time.

So before you get married, Lofas suggests sitting down with your future wife to discuss your ideas about what a family is and represents. Think about your own family while growing up and during your previous marriage. Write down what you liked, what you thought was important, what worked and didn't work. Share notes. Then decide what goals you want to achieve for your new family. Your house rules need to reflect those goals.

Whose Money Is It?

If you're thinking about getting married, have you talked with your partner about finances? More specifically, what debts and assets you're each bringing to the marriage? And if the marriage doesn't work out, is she entitled to your savings, stocks, pension or 401(k)? Are you entitled to hers?

Money is often a difficult issue for any couple to discuss. Talk of prenuptial agreements, bad debt, budgets, high credit card balances or even differences in spending philosophies can sometimes send a relationship into a tailspin, with little room for recovery. Still, it's a discussion that must be had, says Jerry Gale, a licensed marriage and family therapist and professor of family therapy at the University of Georgia in Athens.

"Financial issues are relevant whether you're bringing in $250 a week or $5,000 a week," says Gale, whose school recently developed a model program called, Relational Financial Therapy. Couples receive five sessions with a team of financial counselors and therapists to help them deal with financial issues.

Discussions like these will help you organize what you can and can't do. Gale says both of you will soon have a shared relationship with finances without knowing each other's strengths, weaknesses or preferences. She may be better than you at balancing the checkbook or paying bills. But you may be better at saving or prefer separate checking accounts. One of you may have a big bank account, saving the money for retirement. But your partner may think like a Nike commercial – do, or in this case, spend, all you can now.

Perhaps you're considering a prenuptial agreement. You may have been burned during your first divorce, losing nearly everything. It took many years for you to accumulate your current assets so you're more protective now, not only for yourself, but also your children.

However, talking about prenups requires a great deal of sensitivity. The way you approach the topic can make all the difference between reaching an understanding or causing hurt feelings.

Gale suggests saying something like this: "I'm going into this marriage with all sincerity and optimism that it will be until death do us part. But I've been burned in the past. It was very hard to accrue the assets that I have. I need to have this prenup because of the hurt and pain I've gone through in the past. Hopefully, we will never have to use it. It's a fall back in case things do not go well. I'm doing it to protect myself but would also like you to do one in a way that will protect you."

If you're like most people, you'll be uncomfortable initiating this conversation. So let a financial advisor or even a couples' therapist introduce the topic and help both of you explore alternatives. Gale says before you enter matrimony, you need to be real clear about "what's mine, what's hers and what's ours".

It ain't easy

Being a good step dad isn't about coming on strong or taking a backseat. It's a huge commitment, an enormous undertaking and major life change for everyone in your new family. The more educated you are about the do's and don'ts, the more strategies you learn and apply, the sooner your stepchildren can regard you as a mentor, friend or supportive adult.

Yvonne Kelly, a licensed social worker in private practice at The Step and Blended Family Institute, Ontario, Canada, and certified family coach with the Step Family Foundation, Inc., offers the following tips that can help you develop strong relationships with your stepchildren:

1. Be yourself. Let them get to know the real you. If you're faking it or trying to be someone else, they pick up on that. Kids recognize and appreciate authenticity.

2. Focus on the relationship. Start off by being their friend or mentor, not a parental figure. Kids don't want their new step dad to jump right into the parenting role, especially if their biological father is still alive. They generally resent step dads who overstep that boundary. So ease into this new role.

3. Find shared activities. Look for ways to connect. Ask your stepchildren what they enjoy doing, then engage them in those activities. You don't have to like everything they do. What's important is that you start spending time with them, learn about each other, start caring about each other and begin to build a relationship.

4. Earn their respect. Make respect a key component of your relationship with them. It comes in the form of listening, understanding and taking time out for them when they're ready and need you.

5. Don't personalize the behavior of the children. Initially, most stepparents are not warmly received. Their resistance to you or lack of respect may involve fear and uncertainty. It doesn't mean that disrespectful behavior goes unaddressed. Just don't personalize it, which causes distress, mainly for you.

6. Be responsible for your own reactions, feelings and behaviors. Otherwise, you'll blame your step kids for any unhappiness in your life, which will interfere with the relationship you have with them and their mother.

7. Make your own children feel secure. Knowing that you're doing your best for your kids will minimize your feelings of guilt and even resentment over spending time with your stepchildren when you aren't spending time with your own kids.

8. Recognize that your expectations may be unrealistic. There are no "should be's" or templates for relationships with step kids. Every relationship is different.

9. Don't force yourself or be pressured to love them. This usually backfires. If love or a loving bond is going to occur, it will happen

naturally, over time. If not, you can still enjoy a good relationship with them as a friend or mentor.

10. Don't rush the relationship. Be patient. Allow it to evolve naturally. Just keep paying attention to their basic needs.

11. Define your role as stepfather. Discuss your role with your partner. Make sure you're both on the same page. Then care for your step kids, be there for them and have their best interests at the center of your decisions and behaviors.

12. Think back to your childhood. Put yourself in their position. What frustrated you, angered you, upset you? Understand they've been through a lot, which can explain their behaviors and help pave the road to acceptance and tolerance.

13. Get help if you're still struggling. Read books, hire a coach or find a therapist. Otherwise, your frustration will grow and be taken out on everyone around you. There is no shame in asking for help. This is unknown territory for all stepparents. All stepdads who've been there know how they've benefited from good information and support.

14. Recognize how you contribute to their lives. You have much to offer. Give yourself credit and appreciation even when no one else has noticed.

"Step dads are really well-intentioned," Kelly says. "They just don't have the tools. The things that step kids do that are really difficult and make it challenging for you are often the things you can learn from. They can be your greatest teachers."

Charlie

During the 1980s, Charlie learned many lessons from his 16 year-old stepson. Roughly two years after Charlie remarried, his stepson moved into his home while his stepdaughter lived away at college.

That's when the real trouble began. He says his wife's ex-husband was very angry with her for divorcing him, physically threatened her and often played the role of victim.

"That has a tremendous impact on how able kids are to accept you - the step dad - and integrate into your new unit," says Charlie, now a 71 year-old consultant and M3 member. "As you begin to make inroads with step kids, they get anxious. They tend to take two steps forward and one step backward

because they're feeling they're abandoning their father. Their own positive feelings toward you are compromised by their loyalty to their father."

His stepson began acting out, doing everything from vandalism and selling drugs to drinking and driving. Charlie, who had two daughters with his first wife, says he didn't know how to raise a boy. He and his wife often argued about how to handle her son, which almost destroyed their marriage. Charlie refers to their relationships as a triangle---everyone was in his or her own corner.

This proved to be the ultimate test of his relationship with his new wife. Although the core of their relationship was strong, he says the stress alone was causing serious damage so the couple sought therapy.

That's where they learned the importance of presenting a unified front, ranging from support to discipline and tough love, says Charlie, explaining that this strategy prevented his stepson from driving a wedge between them. He could no longer play one parent against the other.

His stepson managed to graduate high school. Shortly after, Charlie says his wife realized that if he didn't move out of the house, their marriage would be in great jeopardy. So she found her son a summer job as a lifeguard at a university that was miles away from home.

Perhaps being independent or on his own forced his stepson to mature. Maybe it was being away from home that made him appreciate his mother and stepdad. Likewise, once the threat of losing his marriage disappeared, Charlie learned to control his temper with his stepson, empathized more about his situation and periodically stepped back to gain perspective. Best of all: No more triangle. For the first time, Charlie and his stepson began building a relationship.

His stepson, who is now 46 years-old living in another state, still has residual issues. Charlie says he hasn't let go of his anger toward his biological father – who has since passed away—for emotionally neglecting him but has a very close relationship with his mother. As for Charlie, the stepson perceives him as a supportive male, mentor and friend.

Unfortunately, Charlie says he was only able to develop a superficial relationship with his stepdaughter who also lives out-of-state and shares some of the personality characteristics of her biological father. But he says his own two daughters "absolutely love my wife".

As Charlie experienced, there are many variables beyond a step dad's control that can influence the direction of his relationship with his stepchildren. The process alone of forming new relationships and building a new home can be overwhelming and emotionally charged. Looking back, Charlie points at the instability of his stepson's father as the root cause for many of his stepson's issues and their previous relationship issues.

Likewise, he believes the expression, "Love will solve all," is just an illusion. Considering that each family is very different and faces unique challenges that others may not experience, there isn't a universal roadmap that stepdads can follow. What may work for one may be disastrous for another. He believes new stepdads must educate themselves by reading books, joining support groups or participating in therapy to learn effective ways to help raise their stepchildren.

"The Brady Bunch is not likely to work," says Charlie. "You can't force connections. By and large, the more you try to force one big happy family, the more likely it is to backfire."

Marriage Quiz

Thinking about getting remarried? Answer the following questions to see how ready you are for your next committed relationship.

1. Are you and ex-wife still talking about who did what to whom?
2. Are you able to see your role in the failure of your last marriage?
3. Since your divorce, have you spent your time on the hunt for your next sexual conquest?
4. Do your feelings of loneliness overwhelm you at times?
5. Do you hate being single?
6. Do you long to find someone who can understand and support you?
7. Is your life on hold until you find someone you can share it with?
8. Are you suspicious about why someone would want to remarry?
9. Have you learned to love and appreciate yourself?
10. Are you able to enjoy your life and where you are now?

11. Are you guarded with people of the opposite sex?
12. Have you forgiven your ex-wife?
13. Have you learned valuable lessons from your divorce and grown to the point where you're now a better person than you were during your previous marriage?
14. Do you have the emotional resources to give others?

If you've answered, "yes" to questions 2, 9, 10, 12, 13 and 14, give yourself one point for each response. Then give yourself one point for each response if you answered "no" to the remaining questions. If you scored more than 10 points, you're ready to start thinking about remarriage. If you scored nine or below, you probably need more time to grow and heal.

Source: Brett Williams, licensed marriage and family therapist, Costa Mesa, Calif., www.abetterrelationship.net

---

Crash Course

Every now and then - when you feel like pulling your hair out - you may need to revisit the basics of being a good step dad. Consider the following tips as a refresher course when things seem to be getting out-of-hand or not moving as fast as you would like:

- Relationships need to evolve and be developed. They are not instant.
- A blended family involves many adjustments on everybody's part. It is hard, but it is worth it.
- Strive to become more of a friend to your stepchildren - you are not their parent. Trying to be their father immediately sets up conflict or loyalty issues between you and their biological father. It's less confusing to stepchildren if their mother disciplines them, assigns chores or makes decisions about going to a party. But be sure to voice your opinion to your wife in private and discuss your differences. This approach respects the position of the biological father and enables a smoother transition for the blended family. As time goes on, you'll be in a good position to provide increasing influence through the positive relationship you've built with them.
- Develop a relationship with the child that allows for influence rather than control.

- Offer your observations about the child to your new wife, but only if she wants or is ready to hear it. Do it discretely (not in front of the child) and with respect.
- Your new wife is parenting the way she knows how and will be sensitive to criticism. So be supportive and constructive in your message.
- Good communication is the vehicle for conflict resolution and positive change. Focus more on listening than speaking. Ask a lot of questions to better understand.
- Don't forget the marital relationship, especially since it is the hub of the family. It can get easily get lost in daily demands.

Source: R. Phillip Colon, Ph.D., NY-based psychologist who specializes in couples and family counseling and author of *The Apprenticeship to Love: A Field Guide for Finding Love that Works for Life,* www.drphilcolon. com

Trivia:

- The median number of years before people remarry is about three
- The median duration of second marriages that end in divorce is about seven years
- In 2004, 12% of men and 13% of women married twice
- Three percent of both men and women marry three or more times

Resources:

eHow
How to see a Pre-Marriage Counselor
http://www.ehow.com/how_2099841_see-premarriage-counselor.html

Getting Married? 6 Great Reasons to Get Premarital Counseling
http://family-marriage-counseling.com/mentalhealth/getting-married-6-great-reasons-to-get-premarital-counseling.htm

www.divorceandchildren.com
A website that offers tips and a free monthly newsletter on issues related to blended families, alienation, coping with children after a divorce and more.

Everything you need to know about prenuptial agreements
http://www.bankrate.com/brm/prenup.asp

Saying 'I do' to pre-nups may be a smart money move
http://www.bnd.com/542/story/793915.html

10 Tips for Marriage After Divorce
http://psychology.suite101.com/article.cfm/10_tips_for_marriage_after_divorce

Post-Divorce Relationships
Website features a brief article and approximately 100 different resources, everything from step families to parenting classes
http://www.divorcepeers.com/post-divorce-relationships.htm

How to Build a Healthy Relationship With Your Stepchild
http://www.successfulstepfamilies.com/view/5

Family Education Message Boards
http://forums.familyeducation.com/forum

Step Parenting: Become the Best Step Parent You Can Be
http://www.parenting-child-development.com/step-parenting.html

Listing of over 20 resources for Step Families
http://www.dmoz.org/Home/Family/Parenting/Step_Parents/

ABOUT THE AUTHOR

CAROL PATTON EARNED a master's degree in counseling from Oakland University in Rochester, Mich. However, her career interests shifted to writing as she began freelancing for a variety of publications. More than 15 years later, she has written several business guidebooks and over 1,000 published articles on a wide variety of topics for newspapers, websites and national magazines.

She currently lives in Las Vegas, NV, with her husband, Jimmy, and dog, Mozart.